D0773004

ST. FRANCIS OF ASSISI PREACHING TO THE BIRDS

From the painting by Aubin Hervier

SAINTS AND HEROES

To the End of the Middle Ages

BY

GEORGE HODGES

WITH ILLUSTRATIONS

Essay Index Reprint Series

BOOKS FOR LIBRARIES PRESS, INC.
FREEPORT, NEW YORK

First published 1911
Reprinted 1967

LIBRARY OF CONGRESS CATALOG CARD NUMBER:

67-26749

PRINTED IN THE UNITED STATES OF AMERICA

CONTENTS

	PAGE
CYPRIAN, 200-258	3
ATHANASIUS, 296-373	15
AMBROSE, 340-397	27
CHRYSOSTOM, 347-407	41
JEROME, 340-420	56
AUGUSTINE, 354-430	68
BENEDICT, 480-543	87
GREGORY THE GREAT, 540-604 . .	99
COLUMBA, 521-597	113
CHARLEMAGNE, 742-814 . . .	126
HILDEBRAND, 1020-1085 . . .	138
ANSELM, 1033-1109	151
BERNARD, 1091-1153	166
BECKET, 1118-1170	182
LANGTON, 1170-1228	199
DOMINIC, 1170-1221	209
FRANCIS, 1182-1226	219
WYCLIFFE, 1320-1384	234
HUS, 1373-1415	248
SAVONAROLA, 1452-1498 . . .	258

ILLUSTRATIONS

St. Francis of Assisi Preaching to
the Birds . . *Frontispiece*

PAGE

St. Ambrose 27

St. Chrysostom and Other Saints . 41

St. Jerome 56

St. Augustine, with His Mother . 68

St. John and St. Benedict . . 87

Gregory the Great . . . 99

Columba 113

Charlemagne . . . 126

Anselm 151

Virgin and St. Bernard . . . 166

Becket 182

Langton 199

St. Dominic 209

Wycliffe 234

John Hus 248

Savonarola 258

SAINTS AND HEROES

To the End of the Middle Ages

CYPRIAN

200-258

Just about the time when Cyprian was born in Carthage, Perpetua and Felicitas amazed the people. Everybody was talking about it.

Perpetua was twenty-two years old. Cyprian's father and mother must have known her very well. The two families belonged to the same high-born and wealthy society. They were all pagans together. But Perpetua had become a Christian. It was as if, in Russia, the daughter of a noble family should become an anarchist.

She joined the Christians. Then spies broke in upon a secret meeting. She and her companions were brought before the court; and they were all sentenced to be tortured till they changed their minds, or died. Felicitas, one of the company, was a slave girl. Many of the Christians belonged to the slave class. The new religion was largely recruited from the poorest people. The fact made Perpetua's association with them so much the more monstrous. Perpetua's family and friends implored her to renounce her Christian faith. They brought her little baby and begged her, for the child's sake, to sacrifice to the gods, and come home. But she refused. The young men who were arrested with her were thrown to the lions. Perpetua and Felicitas were tossed by a wild cow, and finally killed by the gladiators.

Amidst such scenes, Cyprian was born in Carthage. In his childhood, the Christians were still in constant peril. They were daily liable to insult, hooting, and stoning in the streets. The emperor Septimius Severus made it a crime under the law to invite anybody to join the Christian society. There was even a proposition to deny to the Christians the right of decent burial.

Then the emperors became too busy with other matters to pay much further attention to the spread of Christianity. Some of them were occupied with vicious pleasures, some with civil strife, some with the increasing dangers of barbarian invasion. There was a long peace. Maximin, indeed, broke it in 235; but otherwise it extended from the beginning of the young manhood of Cyprian till he was of an age of between fifty-five and sixty years.

When the persecution began again, in 249, in the reign of Decius, Cyprian himself had become a Christian.

He had first chosen the profession of the law, and attained a wide reputation for his eloquence, and had become a senator. He was rich both by his own efforts and by his family inheritance and lived handsomely in a great house, in the midst of extensive grounds. He had the esteem of his fellow citizens. He seemed to be in possession of all that makes life pleasant. He had reachèd the age of forty-five, when one is easily contented with a comfortable estate, and indisposed to change.

About that time he wrote a letter to his friend Donatus. "Donatus,"—he said, in effect,—"this is a cheerful world indeed as I see it from my fair garden, under the shadow of my vines. But if I could ascend some high mountain, and look out over the wide lands, you know very well what I should see: brigands on the highways, pirates on the seas, armies fighting, cities burning, in the amphitheaters men murdered to please applauding crowds, selfishness and cruelty and misery and despair under all roofs. It is a bad world, Donatus, an incredibly bad world. But I have discovered in the midst of it a company of quiet and holy people who have learned a great secret. They have found a joy which is a thousand times better than any of the pleasures of our sinful life. They are despised and persecuted, but they care not: they are masters of their souls. They have overcome the world. These people, Donatus, are the Christians,—and I am one of them."

Cyprian was baptized. Within a year, he was ordained. Within another year, the bishop of Carthage died, and Cyprian was chosen in his place. The choice was made by the Christian people. They demanded Cyprian. They besieged his house, shouting his name. They gave him no peace till he consented. Thus he became, as the title ran, the Pope of Carthage.

Then arose the Decian persecution.

The thousandth year of the history of Rome had been celebrated with triumphal games, and the emperor Decius was resolved to make the empire great again as it had been of old. But two things were necessary: one was the favor of the gods, the other was the unity of the people. And both of these were contradicted by the Christians. They not only refused to worship the gods, but daily reviled them; and they were a mysterious society, having their own purposes, keeping themselves apart from their neighbors. Plainly the first step toward a renewal of the old strength and glory of Rome was to put an end to the Christians.

Thus began the first general persecution. For almost a hundred years the Christians had lived in peril of their lives. Now in this city and now in that, they had been chased through the streets by mobs, and flung to lions and fire in the arena. But, at the command of Decius, the whole might of the Roman Empire was arrayed against them. In all places, Christians were thrust into prisons, scourged, starved, beaten with forks of iron, driven into the mountains and the deserts. In Rome, in Jerusalem, in Antioch, the bishop died a martyr.

The persecution made two significant disclosures.

It showed, on the one side, how great a place the Christian religion had come to hold in the lives of the people. For the sake of it, they despised death. They withstood the whole force of the imperial power. They declared that they were Christians, and no torture could make them deny their faith. The storm raged for more than a year, and when, in 251, Decius fell in battle fighting against the Goths, and the persecution ceased, the Christians were not defeated. They had suffered untold distresses, but the endeavor to destroy them had failed.

On the other side, the persecution disclosed an unexpected weakness. The long peace which preceded it had brought into the Church a great number of persons who had brought their sins along with them. That quiet and holy company which Cyprian had described to Donatus had come to contain men and women without any real understanding of religion, led astray by avarice and evil temper and offenses of the flesh, and ministered to by priests and even by bishops who were neglectful of their duties, and examples of evil rather than of good. When the persecution fell, these bad Christians, and a still greater crowd of weak ones, appeared immediately. They renounced their religion. They sacrificed to idols. The pagan altars were crowded with throngs of Christians in desperate haste to forsake Christ.

When the persecution was over the Church was confronted with two serious problems.

The first problem concerned the proper treatment of those who had denied the faith. A great number of these weak and frightened people who had deserted their reli-

gion desired to return. What should be done
about them? Some proposed to meet them
with charity, and welcome such as were
really ashamed and sorry, with all loving
kindness. Others proposed to meet them
with severity, and were reluctant to take
them back on any terms whatever. Let
them wait for the everlasting verdict of
God.

The second problem arose from the increasing bitterness with which this debate
was carried on. The advocates of severity
refused to yield anything to the advocates
of charity. And when the charitable people won the day in the decisions of Christian assemblies, the severe people declared
that they would not belong to a church
which could deal with mortal sin so lightly.
They went apart by themselves, and chose
their own bishops and made their own
laws. Thus to the question, What shall
we do with those who have denied the
faith? was added the question, What shall

we do with those who have separated from the Church?

Cyprian came back from the safe place which had sheltered him during the storm of persecution and met these difficult problems. To his clear, legal mind, trained in the conduct of Roman administration, the need of the moment was a strong, central authority. As regarded the lapsed, he was on the side of charity. How could he be otherwise who, in fear or in prudence, had concealed himself from the perils of martyrdom? But as regarded the separatists, he took the position to which his experience as a Roman lawyer inclined him. He maintained the authority of the Church. There is only one church, he said, and outside of it is no salvation. "Whoever he is and wherever he is, he is not a Christian who is not in the Church of Christ." And the Church, he said, consists of those who obey the regularly appointed bishop. "The bishop is in the Church, and the Church is in the bishop, and if any one is not with the bishop, he is not with the Church." The statements are important, because they are the first clear utterances of a new era. They mark the definite beginning of the Church as a factor of essential importance in the Christian religion.

Then the persecution under Decius was followed by a persecution under Valerian.

The attack of Decius had been directed against all Christians; the attack of Valerian was directed mainly against the clergy. The idea was that if the leaders were taken away the Christian societies would fall into confusion. Thus, in Carthage, the storm fell on Cyprian. He made no attempt to escape. He was arrested, and brought to the court through streets lined with people, Christian and pagan. "Your name is Cyprian?" asked the proconsul. "It is," "You are the pope of a sacrilegious sect?" "I am." "The emperors require you to offer sacrifice." "I refuse to do so."

Thereupon the inevitable sentence was pronounced. "Thanks be to God!" said Cyprian.

He was led to the place of execution, the whole city attending. There was no pagan shouting. The man of blameless life and devotion to the good of others had won the esteem and affection of his neighbors. He took off his red cloak, and knelt in prayer. He directed that twenty-five pieces of gold should be given to the executioner. Then he bowed his head, and the ax descended.

ATHANASIUS
296-373

ONE day, in Alexandria, a bishop was standing by a window in his house, which looked out over the sea. He had invited some people to dinner, and they were late in coming, and he was waiting. When they came they found the bishop so interested in what he saw out of the window that they looked also. On the shore of the sea a little group of boys were "playing church." One was the minister, the others were the congregation. The boy who was the minister called up the others one by one and baptized them in the sea; and this he did just as it was done in church, saying the right words and doing the right acts: The bishop beckoned to the boy. "What is your name?" he said. And the boy answered, "Athanasius."

Some years after, when Athanasius had come to the last year of school, the bishop took him into his own house, and he became his secretary, and the bishop loved him as a son. The lad desired to be a minister in earnest, and the bishop taught him, and at last ordained him.

Now the minister of the largest church in Alexandria was named Arius. He was a tall, pale man, careless in his dress, and with his hair tumbling about his head, but kind and pleasant to everybody whom he met, and a great preacher. His church was always crowded, and he was much admired for his goodness and his eloquence. But Arius and the bishop did not agree. And one time, in the presence of a large number of ministers, at a convention, Arius said aloud and publicly that the bishop was not a good teacher of religion. The bishop, he said, was seriously mistaken.

Alexandria, at that time, was much like Athens when it was visited by St. Paul.

It was a place where the people loved to argue and debate.

Now, there are two quite different things about which men may argue. They may debate matters which can be decided by weights or measures; as, for example, the height of a house. And they may come to a speedy decision about which there is no further doubt. Or they may debate matters which nobody understands or can ever understand completely; as, for example, the question whether human beings have any existence before they are born. Here one may say, "Yes, the soul of each man has always been in the world, now in a tree, now in a lion, and, at last, in the man"; while another may say, "No, the soul and the body come into being at the same time." And such a question they may go on debating forever, because neither can prove his position. The Alexandrians were fond of discussing these hard problems. They were, therefore, greatly interested in the debate between Arius and the bishop, and everybody took part in it, on one side or on the other.

Arius said to the bishop, "You teach that Christ is only another name for God, and that there is no difference. How can that be, when God is the Father and Christ is the Son? Is not the Son different from the Father? Is He not, indeed, inferior to the Father? There must have been a time in the far spaces of eternity when the Son began to be, when He was created like the rest of us. He is, of course, divine but in an inferior position." At this the bishop was filled with horror and declared that Arius was either making Christ a creature like man, or at least was robbing Him of so much of His greatness that He was not truly divine, or was setting such a difference between Him and God that there were two gods according to his teaching, two distinct Gods.

This is not the place in which to discuss

this difficult matter, as they discussed it in Alexandria. This much, however, may be said, that Arius in taking the names "Father" and "Son" literally, and making such inferences from them, was putting Christianity in danger of a pagan invasion. For if there may be two distinct gods, the Father and the Son, why not twenty, why not two hundred? We have to remember that a great part of all the people of Alexandria and everywhere else were pagans, and believed in many gods. Out of this the Christians had been saved. They had daily evidence of the confusion and doubt and evil living into which that belief brought men. Thus the doctrine of Arius, while to some it seemed reasonable enough, to others was an attack upon the very central meaning of religion.

The emperor of the Roman world, at that moment, was a Christian. Constantine was the first Christian emperor. One day, as he was crossing the Alps at the head of an army, on his way to fight for that Roman throne which he presently won, he saw a bright light in the sky, like a blazing cross. And that night, in a dream, he saw Christ coming to him and telling him to go to battle with the cross upon his banner. Then when he was victorious, and was made at last sole ruler of the world, he took the side of Christianity. He stopped the long series of bitter persecutions. He put an end to the effort which had been made by emperor after emperor to destroy the Church. He became, in a way, a Christian; though not a particularly good one.

So when the debate which Arius began spread from Alexandria to other cities and threatened to divide the Christians into contending armies, Constantine interfered. One of his great hopes in siding with the Christians was thereby to bring about the unity of the people; and here were the Christians themselves divided. He determined to stop it by calling a great Christian council to decide the question.

The appointed place was Nicæa, near to where Constantine soon founded the city of Constantinople. To Nicæa, then, came bishops from all parts of the empire, from Carthage and Italy and Spain in the West, from India and Persia in the East. Some were lame and some were blind after the tortures of the persecutions. The president for the eastern churches was Eusebius of Nicomedia, the president for the western churches was Hosius of Cordova. All Christendom was represented. With the bishop of Alexandria came Athanasius.

The purpose of the council was to present to the world a statement of the true belief of Christians concerning the nature of Christ. This they did in terms which were afterwards used in what is

called the Nicene Creed. Arius refused
to sign it, and a few others agreed with
him. They were expelled from the
Church. Then the council was disbanded,
and Constantine and everybody else
thought that the trouble was happily
ended. As a matter of fact, it was only
begun.

No sooner had the bishops returned to
their homes than the contention arose
anew. Some liked the Nicene decision;
others, as they considered it further, were
not satisfied. And the unsatisfied ones
were influential at the court. One was
the chaplain of the emperor. Constantine
was thus persuaded that Arius was right,
after all. And what Constantine thought
was the immediate opinion of many who
knew little about it but were very anxious
to stand well with Constantine. Against
these Arians was Athanasius. Old Bishop
Alexander had now died, and Athanasius
had been made bishop in his place.

The dispute became a struggle between Alexandria and Constantinople, between Athanasius and Constantine. Arius himself presently died. He had been received by the emperor, and an order was issued that he should be restored to the communion of the Church. The old man was actually on his way to the service when he was seized with a bitter pain, so that he stopped in the street and sought refuge in the nearest house. The triumphal procession waited for him at the door. At last a man came out and said that Arius was dead. Constantine too came to the end of his great life, but his sons who succeeded him were on the Arian side.

Athanasius was banished from his city, and came back only to be banished again. Once on his return the rejoicings were so great that in after years, when the youth of Alexandria praised the splendor of any festival, the old men said,

"Yes, but you should have been here on the day when Pope Athanasius came home."

Troops were sent to Alexandria. Athanasius was besieged in the church where he was holding service. It was in the night, and the great church, crowded with worshipers, was dimly lighted with lamps. The soldiers broke down the doors, and with drawn swords made their way through the congregation, in the midst of wild disorder, to the chancel. Athanasius was rescued by his friends after being nearly torn in pieces. He escaped to the desert.

One time he was pursued by his enemies on the Nile. As he rounded a bend of the river, in the dusk, he ordered his rowers to turn back. His pursuers came on with all haste and in the dusk of the late afternoon the two boats met. "Have you seen Athanasius?" the soldiers called across the water. "Yes," replied the bishop,

" he is not far away! " Thus he escaped
again.

This life of hardship and danger
Athanasius lived because he was not willing to deny what he held to be the faith.
The whole Church seemed to be against
him. Council after council was called by
the emperors, attended by hundreds of
bishops, making Arian creeds. The whole
empire was thrown into confusion.
Athanasius, on the other side, was preaching sermons and writing books and letters.
The one man defied the Church. And he
gained the victory! Year by year, it
became plain that the theology of Arius
was filled with confusion. People were
perplexed by a long series of different
Arian statements of belief. Athanasius
maintained the divinity of Christ, in
whom God dwelt among men. People
were dismayed at the energy with which
the Arian court used the swords of soldiers
to maintain its side. The Church grew

weary of the fierce debate. Then the
last of the Arian emperors fell in battle
with the Goths, and the war was ended.
Theodosius, who followed him, was of
the faith of Athanasius.

ST. AMBROSE

From a mural painting, Castle of Karlstein, Bohemia

of their ancestors. They loved the customs which were glorified in the literature and sculpture of old Rome. They felt toward the Christians as people of long descent and gentle breeding are tempted to feel to-day toward new neighbors, rich but ill-educated, with new ways.

The senate, therefore, petitioned for the return of the Altar of Victory. The humble terms of their request showed how completely the old era of pagan power had passed. They asked only for permission to keep a few of the ancient ceremonies and to say their own prayers in their own way. " Let us have one altar out of the destruction of the old religion. Pestilence and famine are abroad, and the barbarians are pressing down across the Danube and the Rhine; let us who are still of the old faith implore the protection of the gods who in the ancient days saved Rome when the Goths besieged it."

Against this petition Ambrose protested.
The gods, he said, had nothing to do with
the saving of old Rome; it was the geese
whose cackling waked the guard. And the
altar was not replaced.

But the conflict was not over. In Alexandria, the Christians and the pagans fell to
fighting, as they fought in the days of the
persecutions; but now the pagans were on
the defensive. The Christians attacked the
mighty pagan temple, the Serapium, high
on vast stone terraces in the midst of the
city, approached by an ascent of a hundred
steps. In the shrine stood the great image
of Serapis, at whose fall, men said, the
world itself would fall. Up went the victorious Christians, clambering with clubs
and axes over the hundred steps, and breaking at last into the splendid shrine. Here
they stopped, and for a little space nobody
dared to proceed further. What if the
ancient legend should prove true, and
Serapis should avenge the insult to his

image by earthquake, and lightning, and destruction! At last a soldier raised his ax and struck the idol full in the face. The cheek of Serapis was broken, and out swarmed a troop of frightened mice whose nest in the idol's head had been thus invaded. Then the silence of the destroyers changed to great laughter and shouts of derision; the image was pulled down and dragged about the streets. And there was no more public paganism in Alexandria.

In the West, the conflict came to an end in a mountain battle beside the Frigidus. The pagans had chosen a pagan emperor, and he went out at the head of an army to fight with Theodosius, not only for his throne, but for his religion. As they passed Milan, the pagans promised that when they returned they would stable their horses in the church of Ambrose. Thus the battle was joined; a fierce storm of snow beat in the faces of the pagan army, and they fled in hopeless defeat. It was the last stand of the old religion.

Meanwhile, Ambrose was contending with the Arians. There were not many of them in Milan, and they were discouraged by the gradual and general failure of their cause; but they had the Empress Justina on their side. She was the mother of the young emperor of whose domains, in the division of the empire, Milan was the capital. The Arians had been turned out of their churches, as the pagans had been turned out of their temples. But Justina was an Arian still. She asked the permission of Ambrose to have for herself and those who were of her belief, a single church in Milan. Ambrose refused to give it.

The long fight of the Arians against the Nicene Creed had been fought and lost. It had filled the Church with clamor and bitterness and division and tragedy. Now it was ended, and Ambrose would give no opportunity for beginning it again. He told the empress that she could not have a church. The empress, thereupon, proposed to take one. She had her imperial soldiers, and she gave them orders to drive Ambrose out of the city and to seize such churches as she wished. The bishop took refuge in a church, and his people gathered about him. There they guarded him day and night, passing the time in singing psalms.

At last, the bishop had a dream. He dreamed that beneath another church two martyrs of some old persecution had been buried. So men went to the place and dug into the ground with spades, and there, sure enough, they came upon the bones of these forgotten saints! And immediately the saints' bones began to work the most astonishing miracles. The lame were made to walk, and the blind to see. The whole city was filled with new excitement. It was plain, men said, that heaven and the saints were on the side of Ambrose. In the face of such reinforcements the empress prudently retreated. Thus was fought the last battle with the Arians in Milan.

The Roman emperors, after Constantine, were most of them weak rulers, sometimes quite young men, like Constantine's own sons, and, for the most part, governing only a portion of the empire. It was divided into east and west, with an emperor for each division; and each of these divisions was parted into imperial provinces. But there was one strong emperor, who in his time ruled the world. That was the great Theodosius.

But Theodosius had a hasty temper, and it brought him into a memorable conflict with Ambrose.

The people of that time were tremendously interested in athletic games. They went in great crowds to the vast amphitheaters where gladiators fought, and the circuses where chariot races were run. One side was for the Blues, the other for the Greens. In every city these sports brought together thousands of spectators.

Now it happened that in Thessalonica, a very popular charioteer had committed a crime, and had very properly been put in prison for it. The time for the races approached, and there was the charioteer still in the prison, and with no likelihood of release. The people, for the sake of the race, demanded of the governor that he should pardon the charioteer and let him out. But the governor refused. Thereupon a mob arose. They attacked the governor's house, and killed him, and dragged his body about the streets; and they released the charioteer.

Tidings of these disorders came speeding to the ear of Theodosius. The murdered governor had been his intimate friend. His anger knew no bounds. Straight he sent messengers to a commander of his troops with orders to avenge this tragedy upon the whole people of Thessalonica. The soldiers found the races in full swing. The immense circus was crowded to the topmost seat. The avengers entered, closed the gates and drew their swords, and proceeded to kill everybody in sight. For three hours they murdered the unarmed people. Seven thousand men, women, and children fell before them.

The story is still remembered of a father who had taken his two boys to the races, and begged the murderers to spare one, and to this they agreed, but he could not decide which one. He could not choose either of his sons to be put to death before his eyes. So the hasty soldiers killed them both, and their father with them.

Ambrose immediately wrote a letter to Theodosius. "You are a Christian," he said, " and have done this horror. Into this has your hasty anger led you. As for me, I pray for you, but you and I cannot stand together in the same church. Do not venture to appear where I am present. You have done the most horrible thing that was ever heard of. Repent before God, ask His pardon as David did. May He be merciful to your sinful soul."

In spite of the letter, the emperor came to church. The bishop met him in the outer porch. "You may not enter," he said. "This is no place for such as you, unless they come in the deepest shame and sorrow. Go back to your palace. Your hands drip with blood. Repent! repent! and then come; but not now."

It is one of the noblest scenes in history. Never has the Church stood out more splendidly against the world. There were later times, as we shall see, when bishops made themselves masters of kings, but sometimes their victory was spoiled by pride and selfishness. The triumph of Ambrose was a triumph of the Christian conscience. He was strong because he was right. And the great emperor knew it. He did repent. He humbled himself before God. In the church, in the presence of the people, he bowed himself to the ground with tears. "My soul cleaveth to the dust," he said. "O God, quicken me according to Thy word." He made a law, which still holds in all civilized countries, that no capital sentence should be carried into effect until thirty days after the condemnation.

Thus in the West, in the person of Ambrose, the Church asserted the rights of man against the injustice and tyranny of the State, and prevailed over the power of kings.

ST. CHRYSOSTOM AND OTHER SAINTS

From the painting by Sebastiano del Piombo, Church of St. Chrysostom, Venice

CHRYSOSTOM

347-407

WHEN the imperial messenger had finished his address to the people of Antioch, there was a profound silence. Nobody said a word. Only in the borders of the crowd could be heard the sobs of frightened women. It was evident that the situation was most serious.

The emperor, the messenger said, is in need of money. He has to keep up a continual war with the miserable barbarians who plunder our unprotected towns, and the soldiers must be paid. You are all rich here. Theodosius lays a new tax on his faithful people, the citizens of Antioch.

Within an hour, the crowd which had listened in ominous silence was a vast mob, yelling in the streets. They attacked the palace of the governor, who happily escaped through the back door, and saved his life. They broke into the great hall of justice. There was the empty seat of judgment, and behind it, against the wall, a row of stately statues: the image of the emperor Theodosius, and of the empress Flacilla, recently dead and tenderly mourned, and of their two sons, Arcadius and Honorius. For an instant the mob stood still, like the crowd in the Shrine of Serapis at Alexandria. Then a boy threw a stone. It struck the figure of the emperor. Instantly, as if it had been the breaking of a spell, rough hands were laid upon the statues. They were pulled down from their places, kicked and struck with clubs, and broken, and the maimed trunks were dragged in the dust of the streets. The trouble lasted two or three hours. Then the soldiers came and took possession. And the people, scattering to their homes, began to consider what they had been about.

The massacre in the circus at Thessalonica had not yet taken place. That was three years in the future. But the furious temper of Theodosius was well known. What would he do? How would he avenge the insult to himself and his family? It was true that one time when he was told that a mob in Alexandria had stoned his statue, he had put his hand to his head, and laughed, saying, " It doesn't hurt." But this was a more serious affair. He might degrade the city from its proud place in the empire and thus destroy its business. He might multiply the tax by ten. He might take off the heads of a hundred leading citizens. He might do this or that. What would he do?

The only hope for Antioch lay in the fact that Theodosius was a Christian. He might listen to the apologies of a Christian bishop. The aged Flavian started, accordingly, in the dead of winter, over eight hundred miles of hard road, with snow lying deep in the passes of the Taurus Mountains, to carry the repentance of Antioch to the emperor at Constantinople.

Meanwhile, the city listened day after day to the sermons of a great preacher.

The name Chrysostom means Golden-mouth, and it was given to a man in Antioch whose other name was John. He had prepared himself for the work of the ministry by years of privation and solitude in the mountains, thinking and praying and listening to the voice of God in his soul. When he came out, he had a burning message to men about their sins. And he feared no living man. He was poor, and preferred to be poor. He asked nothing, except an opportunity to speak. And when he spoke, it was with an eloquence which made his hearers cry or laugh or tremble, as he pleased.

Thus Chrysostom ministered to Antioch

during the long weeks of suspense. He preached daily. He taught to people the uncertainty of all the riches and pleasures of this life, and urged them day by day to store their treasures in heaven, and to lay hold upon that happiness which no chance or change can spoil. At last the bishop came in sight, sending his news ahead to Chrysostom, and he announced it from his pulpit. The emperor had pardoned the suppliant city. He was a Christian, and he was mindful of Christ's great words about forgiveness. Then came the bishop, welcomed with festivities like those at Alexandria, "when Pope Athanasius came home."

Chrysostom had been for ten years the splendid preacher of Antioch when the bishop of Constantinople died. Theodosius had died also, and his weak son, Arcadius, was in his place. The real ruler of the eastern empire was a man named Eutropius.

The career of Eutropius is one of the most singular in history. He had been born a slave, and had passed from one master to another. One of his occupations had been to comb his mistresses' hair. He had grown old and wrinkled and ugly, till nobody would buy him, and he had been turned out of doors, like an old horse. He had found work in the kitchen of the imperial palace, and had made his way from one domestic post to another, till he had become a chamberlain. Being thus near to the emperor's person, he had gained increasing influence over that weak youth, till he secured his amazing success by suggesting that he marry Eudoxia, the daughter of a general of the Franks. Now, the all-powerful courtier and favorite and prime minister, Rufinus, had planned that his own daughter should became the bride of the emperor, and so slyly had Eutropius managed that when the wedding procession actually started out, Rufinus and his daughter waited to meet it in state, till it passed the house of Rufinus and stopped at the house of Eudoxia. That, of course, was the end of Rufinus, and Eutropius took his place. The old slave, who had begged in the streets of Constantinople, had become the right hand and master of the emperor.

Eutropius had once heard Chrysostom preach, and when the bishop of Constantinople lay dead, and the churchmen were eagerly discussing who should sit in his great seat, he sent secret messengers to Antioch, and they stole Chrysostom. They asked him to get into their carriage, and when he was once in, away they drove, at post haste, much against his will, to Constantinople, and there he was made bishop. The bishop of Alexandria, who was much disgusted, having other plans, was forced to consecrate him.

Thus Chrysostom became bishop of

Constantinople, and found himself in the midst of the imperial court.

The first thing which he did was to take all the fine furniture which had belonged to his rich and luxurious predecessor, and put it out in the street, and sell it at auction. He dismissed all the servants. The splendid dinners, for which the bishop's house had been famous, came to a sudden end. The new bishop was as poor as the poorest of his people. All the money which came to him he spent for the relief of the needy and the care of the sick.

Then he preached, as he had done at Antioch, terribly plain sermons about sin; and not about sin in general, but about the actual temptations and sins of the people to whom he spoke. He reproved them for the ways in which they made their money, and for the ways in which they spent it. He reproached them for the cries and groans of their slaves, which he heard from their windows as he passed by in the street. He even criticized the clothes of the ladies. He spared nobody, the court least of all. The proud, luxurious, and selfish life of the emperor and the empress and their friends he disliked exceedingly, and said so plainly.

From the people, he proceeded to speak his mind about the clergy. He found them idle and neglectful of their duties, and called them to account. Some he reproved, some he expelled. Thus every day, by every word he said, he made an enemy. They were enemies of the right kind, who had no place in the friendly approval of a true bishop, but they were many, and some of them were in places of great power. They were able, and more than willing, to do him harm.

Thus the ministry of Chrysostom in Constantinople was very hard. He was as eloquent as ever, and the churches were crowded to hear him, but people went away after the sermon clinching their fists.

At last, the great Eutropius fell from his high place. He presumed too much upon his power over the weak emperor. One day he said to the empress, "I put you on your throne, and I can thrust you down." Eudoxia ran crying to Arcadius, bringing her little children with her, and demanded the expulsion of Eutropius. And the emperor, with most unexpected energy, expelled him. So he fell, and an hour after he was without a friend. He had lost everything except his life. That he saved by running to the cathedral, and clinging to the altar. From that holy place, nobody ventured to drag him out. The bishop protected him. He faced the crowd which clamored for the old man's blood. He interceded for him with the emperor. He got him for a time into a safe exile. Even so, with his instinct for a preacher's occasion, he could not resist taking him for a tremendous text. There was the fallen favorite, in the sight of the congregation, on the floor by the altar, his hair in disorder, his clothes torn, trembling for fear of death. Chrysostom pointed at him from the pulpit. "You see," he said, "how uncertain are all the honors of the world."

Now, the empress Eudoxia had caused to be erected, in the square fronting the cathedral, a statue of herself. It was of silver, on a porphyry column. And on the day when it was set up there was such a clamor outside the church, with dancing and singing, that Chrysostom could scarcely hear himself preach. He expressed his displeasure in his blunt manner, and his words were reported to the empress. It was the crisis of a long hatred. The anger of the court was confirmed by the anger of the clergy. They were all against the righteous bishop, all whose evil lives he had condemned. The bishop of Alexandria had left his own city to trouble Chrysostom. Councils had convened to find some fault in him, like the councils which made false charges against Athanasius. The affair of the silver statue brought the full storm upon his head. Arcadius, whose father, Theodosius, had trembled before Ambrose, ordered Chrysostom into exile. And he had no friends to help him whose strength was of account in such a struggle.

Out he went, then, into exile. And as he went, a black smoke began to rise from the city, and flames beneath the smoke. The cathedral was mysteriously on fire. It was destroyed; and the great houses of government about it joined in its ruins. And beneath the charred and broken beams and stones which filled the square, lay the porphyry pedestal and the silver statue of Eudoxia.

They carried the old man, under a guard of soldiers, the whole length of

Asia Minor, from Constantinople at the northwestern corner to the region above Antioch, in the southeastern corner. It was much the same journey which Bishop Flavian had made when he went to intercede for Antioch with Theodosius. But his place of exile was too near his friends to please his enemies. Letters of sympathy came to him by every mail, from the bishop of Rome, from the bishop of Milan, from bishops of the East who braved the enmity of the court. And every mail carried back letters from Chrysostom to his faithful people in Constantinople, who were suffering for his sake, to bishops and churches asking for his counsel. He speaks of exile and famine, war and pestilence, siege and solitude, as belonging now to his daily life. The place of his exile was bitterly cold in winter, and there were brigands who came down from the mountains to steal and kill. But he kept his courage and his good cheer.

At last an imperial order directed that he should be carried north to the shore of the Black Sea. Chrysostom was ill, and the summer was hot; the journey was long and difficult. The guards who conducted him had been given to understand that if their prisoner should chance to die by the way, it would be to their advantage, they would be paid so much the more. And die, he did. Beside a village in Pontus he sank down and could go no further. They dragged him on, but he was evidently dying. They took him to a little chapel, and there, crying, with his last breath, " Glory be to God for all things! " he passed away.

Chrysostom was as truly a martyr as Cyprian. But the bishop of Carthage had been put to death by pagans; the bishop of Constantinople was put to death by Christians. To this pass had the course of events come in that religion whose disciples had seemed to Cyprian so quiet and holy. While the Church in the West was mastering the evil passions even of emperors, the Church in the East was fighting a losing battle against the sin of the world. After that, in the East, the Court ruled the Church, as it does to this day. There were good and brave men, but the short list of eminent Eastern Saints and Heroes ends with Chrysostom.

The life of Chrysostom differed from the life of Ambrose as defeat differs from victory, but the two men were intent on the same thing. The emphasis of the ministry of Cyprian was upon the Church: he exalted the importance of the Church. The emphasis of the ministry of Athanasius was upon the creed: he magnified the importance of the creed. But the emphasis of the ministry of Ambrose and of Chrysostom was upon the essential and pre-eminent importance of character. That, they said, is the very heart and life of the Christian religion.

JEROME

340-420

WHEN Athanasius fled to Rome, he carried with him two tall monks, straight from the deserts by the Nile. They were lodged in the great house of a noble lady who had a little daughter named Marcella. One of the monks was a very grave and silent person, who spent all his time in Rome at the tombs of St. Peter and St. Paul. But the other had many a story to tell about the wilderness from which he came, and about the monks who lived there. And Marcella listened eagerly.

Even to grown people, the accounts of the monastic life were like the descriptions which travelers give of lands hitherto unknown. In the sandy wastes beside the Nile were men in little huts who had forsaken the world in order to say their

ST. JEROME

From the picture by Ghirlandaio, Church of Ognissanti, Florence

prayers in peace. Some had escaped from the dangers of the pagan persecutions; some had grown weary of the life of cities, or disgusted with the selfishness and cruelty of their neighbors; some had come to believe a new doctrine brought from the East, which said that the human body is the root of all evil and the residence of the devil, and that we must starve it and beat it for the good of the soul; some desired only to be let alone. There were thousands of them, living this strange life.

The monk told how they earned their living by making baskets, and how they ate little, and slept little, and prayed much, and how the wild beasts howled at night, and how wild and still it was on the wide sand and under the wide sky. Marcella felt that that was the most wonderful and happy life in the world. And other Roman people, her elders, felt the same way. The idea of complete independence of the world, of freedom from all the cares of the common day, and of nearness to God, appealed to a great many who were tired; and to some who were penitent for their sins. They said, Why should we not go out into the wastes and woods and be monks, like the holy people of the Nile? But years passed, and most of the men and women lived in the old way, till Jerome came.

Jerome was born in that year when the monks visited Rome. Presently he went there to school, and had for teacher old Donatus, whose Latin grammar was studied by all the schoolboys of Europe from that time forward for twelve hundred years. Jerome was an uncommonly good scholar and his chief delight was to sit down with a book. All his life long, in cities and in deserts, and on journeys, he carried a book with him.

The accounts which he heard of the monks in the East attracted him as they had attracted Marcella. He went into the

East, and entered that life of religious adventure. He became a monk. He found a desert in Syria, near Antioch, where monks were living, and settled down among them.

They used to tell the story of a lion which came one day to Jerome, holding out his paw with a thorn in it, and Jerome took out the thorn, and the lion became his devoted friend. Jerome himself, however, had much more to say about the devil. He said that the devil spoiled all the peace and happiness of his life. He had gone into the desert to get away from the sin of the world, but the temptations to sin followed him. The devil put evil thoughts into his heart.

Once he dreamed that God was angry with him for being so fond of Cicero; in his dream, he was in the other world, and the angels beat him with sticks as his teachers used to do in school; his shoulders in the morning were black and blue. For a good while, he read the Bible instead of Cicero.

But he felt that God was angry with him for much more serious offenses than this. Day by day, he found himself thinking evil thoughts; and day by day, his temper, which had never been very good, grew worse. In trying to live without eating, he injured his health. In short, he met with the difficulties and suffered the pains which come naturally when people treat their bodies badly, and attempt to change the nature with which they were made.

Then he came to Rome, still believing in the kind of life in which he had been so unsuccessful. He devoted himself to teaching it. He became acquainted with Marcella. She was now a woman of forty, and lived in a splendid palace on the Aventine Hill. Jerome had classes in her house. All the girls in Roman society who desired to do better than to live the life of the world attended them. Jerome told them what a wicked world it was, and earnestly advised them not to get married. All the young men in Rome hated him.

The meetings in Marcella's house affected the social life of Rome. Good women came, and brought their friends. The pleasures of society were neglected for these new studies. Nobody went, as yet, into the wilderness to pray, but many prayed and fasted and did their best to live like the monks, at home. Lea founded a convent of holy women. Melania went on a pilgrimage to the holy places in Palestine. Fabiola established a hospital.

The nearest friends of Jerome were the Lady Paula, and her daughters. They belonged, like the other members of this devout company, to the ancient aristocracy of Rome. They had social position, and wealth, and all the honors and luxuries of life. They gave them up to live in the new way. They spent their money in good works, and went about in poor clothes, and fasted.

One of the daughters died. She had been so fond of gaiety, and had so delighted in the pleasant life which, under Jerome's teaching she had given up, the people said she had been killed by the change. They laid the blame on Jerome. At her funeral there was a great indignation, and some proposed to stone the monk or throw him into the Tiber. Finally, when the feeling against Jerome so increased that he was in peril of his life, he left Rome and spent the rest of his days in Bethlehem. Paula and another daughter, Eustochium, went with him. There they built two monasteries, one for themselves and such other women as might join them; the other for Jerome.

The remainder of the life of Jerome

was spent in those studies in which he had
delighted from his youth. In the quiet
of his monastic house, apart from the dis-
tractions of the world, he set about a task
to which we are all in debt to-day. He
translated the Bible into Latin.

The Bible was the first book in the
world to be translated from one language
to another. It was brought over from
Hebrew into Greek. That was done in
Alexandria about two hundred years before the Christian era. The story was that
seventy learned Jews, in seventy separate
cells, turned the Hebrew into Greek in
seventy days, and thus produced seventy
Bibles which were all alike, even,—as the
phrase is,—to the dotting of the *i's* and
the crossing of the *t's*.

But Greek had ceased to hold its old
place as the language of the great world.
St. Paul, indeed, had written a Greek
letter to the Romans, and for many years
all Christian services in Rome had been in

Greek. But two other languages had now appeared.

One was the language of the Goths, spoken in various dialects, by that vast multitude of barbarians who every year were drawing nearer to the Roman empire, until, at last, in Jerome's day, they captured Rome itself. This Teutonic language is of interest to us because it was the parent of our English speech. Into this tongue an Arian bishop, Ulfilas, had already translated a great part of the Bible. It was the first book in all that mighty literature which is now German and English.

The other language was Latin. In Jerome's time, Greek was the language of the past and Gothic was the language of the future, but Latin was the language of the present. Into Latin, then, he translated the Bible. He studied Greek, he studied Hebrew. A friendly rabbi came over from Tiberias by night to teach him.

The work occupied him fifteen years. He dedicated it to his faithful friends, Paula and Eustochium.

From that day to this, the Latin Bible of Jerome has been the authorized version of the Latin Church. The Vulgate, as it is called, is used in the West, as the Greek Bible, the Septuagint, is used in the East. When the Bible was at last translated into English, the translators knew Jerome's Bible by heart. They brought over into our book the splendid cadence of its sentences. Of course, English as we have it now is a combination of those two languages which in Jerome's time were of the present and the future. It is part Gothic and part Latin. But the words of Latin derivation in our English Bible correspond to the Latin words which Jerome chose. They are written over into our Bible out of his.

It is unhappily remembered of Jerome that he was not only a monk and a scholar but a fierce debater. He loved to argue, and when he argued he went about it in the spirit of a fighter. The man with whom he disagreed was, for the moment, his worst enemy, and he treated him accordingly. He looked about for every possible mean thing to say about him. He called him names. He accused him of dishonesty. He said that he was a liar. He insinuated that he was both a fool and a knave.

This method of argument, no matter how well-founded the argument itself may be, always puts the arguer in the wrong. He may have on his side all the truth of the Christian religion, he has the spirit of the devil. It began before Jerome, and continued so long that we have only recently outgrown it. It never did good, nor corrected anybody from the error of his mistaken opinions. The instinctive reply is not to say, "Yes, I see that I was wrong and you are right," but to say,

"Right or wrong, I will hit you back as hard as you hit me."

Jerome was a very abusive and bad-tempered saint. Still, that sort of controversy was the fashion then; though he rather outdid the rest of the wrangling brethren. He knew no other way to show that he was in earnest. And his life in the desert had ruined his digestion.

AUGUSTINE

354-430

AMONG the young men who listened with interest to the eloquence of Ambrose in the cathedral of Milan was one named Augustine. He was an outsider, a pagan, and went to church, not because he was concerned about the Christian religion, but because he liked to hear good speaking. Perhaps, however, he thought sometimes, in the midst of the service and the sermon, of his Christian mother, Monica.

We are told much of the thoughts as well of the acts of Augustine by himself, in his famous " Confessions." This was the first of all the autobiographies. Augustine was the first man in all history to write a book about himself. And this he did with such frankness, and such continual human interest, that it remains

ST. AUGUSTINE, WITH HIS MOTHER

From the picture by Ary Scheffer

to-day the chief autobiography in literature.

Thus we know that he was born in Africa, not far from Carthage, the son of descendants of Latin colonists, like Cyprian. That is, his people were African by residence, but Italian by race. His father was a pagan, and lived the careless, and even evil life which paganism permitted. The one good thing reported of him is that he did not beat his wife; but even that was explained by Monica on the ground that it takes two to make a quarrel.

Augustine says that he was a bad boy at school, getting his lessons pretty well,—though he hated mathematics,—but running away to play ball, and being well whipped for it. As he grew up, he showed an inclination to follow the example of his father rather than the piety of his mother.

He went to college in Carthage, a place full of temptation, into which he fell. He

says, however, that what he most desired
was not the pleasure of sin, but the praise
of his companions. Accordingly, he pre-
tended to be worse than he really was.
One of the lesser offenses of the wild
youths who were his associates in college
was to break up the lectures of the professors. A gang of them would go about,
and rush shouting into classroom after
classroom, destroying all the order of
the college. Still, Augustine studied to
such good purpose that he was asked to
become a teacher himself.

Now he found that the pleasant pastime
of mobbing professors was much more
agreeable to the students than it was to
the professors, and after being put to this
annoyance several times, he gave up in
disgust, and found some teaching to do in
Rome. The students in Rome were much
more polite than in Carthage, but they
had a custom which was almost equally
objectionable. They would attend their

classes with great diligence until just before the time to pay their annual fees; then they would depart and appear no more. As Augustine depended on his fees for his support, this was a serious matter.

Happily, however, at this moment a professorship fell vacant in Milan; it was a position which was supported by the State, with a salary paid from the State treasury. This comfortable place was offered to Augustine by the Roman senator who pleaded against Ambrose for the Altar of Victory. Thus he came to Milan.

He had now learned some lessons under the instruction of experience. He had mastered the worst of his old sins. He had become interested in the discussion of religion: but not in the Christian religion. He had found a sect of people called Manichees, whose creed was brought from Persia. They believed in two gods, like the Persians, a good god and a bad one. They had a long series of secret initiations by which one passed by one degree after another to illumination and perfection. Augustine went a little way in this society, but not far. He was profoundly dissatisfied with the world in which he lived, and with himself.

He began to find what he needed, in the teachings of Ambrose. Ambrose said, " Here is the Church, a divine teacher with truth from heaven. Come into it, all perplexed souls, and take this truth and live according to it, and be at peace." It appealed to Augustine. It seemed a pleasant prospect. But his mind was full of questions. Several times he went to see the bishop. There sat Ambrose in his great hall, with a book in his hand, and people coming to consult him. When there was a space between these visits, he read his book. Augustine hesitated to interrupt his studies. He went away without asking any of his questions.

At last, one day, one of a little group

of Augustine's friends began to tell the story of St. Anthony, the hermit, as it had been written by Athanasius: how he had heard in church about the rich young man to whom the Lord said, " Sell all that thou hast and follow Me;" how he obeyed that command, and took up his lodging in the desert, how he lived there amidst the friendly beasts, saying his prayers, strengthening his soul, and blessed of God. Augustine was profoundly interested. He went away alone into a little quiet garden and flung himself upon the grass. " How long," he cried, " shall I pray ' O God, make me a Christian, but not yet,' —how long shall I be like one who is awakened in the morning and knows that he ought to get up, yet lies in idle dreaming."

Suddenly he heard the voice of a child singing. Over and over the child sang, " Take and read! Take and read!" It seemed to Augustine a message from on high. Immediately he rose up and went into the house and took a Bible, and opened wherever it would open and read the words which there appeared upon the page. The words were, " Not in rioting and drunkenness, not in chambering and wantonness, not in strife and envying; but put ye on the Lord Jesus Christ, and make not provision for the flesh, to fulfil the lusts thereof."

This experience changed his life. He applied to Ambrose for baptism. He devoted himself to the study and the teaching of the Christian religion. He took his mother, and set out to return to Africa. From Milan they went to Rome, and from Rome down the Tiber to the port of Ostia. There they waited for a ship. One evening, as they sat together in the starlight, talking of the past and the future, Monica said, "Augustine, I have now no more to live for. All these years I have prayed for you that you might be a Christian.

Now my prayers are answered." The next day she fell sick, in a little while she died, the patron saint of all devout and patient and long-enduring mothers.

Augustine settled on the farm which had belonged to his father, and gathered friends about him. There they lived, digging occasionally in the garden, but more for exercise than in expectation of crops, and occupying themselves for the most part with quiet talking, and thinking, and reading and writing. One day Augustine went on an errand to the near town of Hippo. There was a service in the parish church, and he attended it. And the bishop saw him in the congregation, and when the time came for the sermon the bishop said, "Brethren, you know that I am getting old, and am in need of help. I am, moreover, a Greek, and it is hard for me to pray in Latin. I ought to have an assistant." Then he looked at Augustine, and everybody looked at Augustine, and there was a great shouting of Augustine's name. There was no help for it; he must be a bishop. By and by the bishop died and Augustine took his place.

Hippo is in Algeria, on a bay which opens into the Mediterranean. The place is much frequented by astronomers on the occasion of a total eclipse of the sun. In the midst of the town is a new cathedral dedicated to St. Augustine, who is still known there, even among the Moslems, as " the great Christian."

The size of the place in which a man lives matters little. The only thing which matters much is the size of the man. Augustine in the little town of Hippo was a person of more consequence and influence than the bishop of Carthage, the bishop of Rome, the bishop of Constantinople, and the bishop of Alexandria put together. He was the greatest man who had appeared in the Christian Church since St. Paul.

Augustine now became acquainted with the meaning of two new words. One word was "schism," the other was "heresy." Schism means separation, and was applied to people who separated themselves from the Church. Heresy means choice, and was applied to people who chose to think for themselves, and came to conclusions different from the common teaching of the creed. These words became important on account of the increasing disorder of the age. The Roman Empire was going to pieces, the hands of government were weak, the invading barbarians were strong, the old order was steadily giving way. It was necessary, under these conditions, to maintain discipline in the Church. There must be leadership and obedience, as in an army in the time of war. The Christians must be kept together. Wise men felt then, as wise men felt afterwards in Massachusetts in the days of the wild Indians, that all differences must be prevented. People must act alike, and think alike, and keep step, for the general safety.

Thus Augustine came into contention with the schism of Donatus, and with the heresy of Pelagius.

The schism of Donatus had now been going on so long that many people had forgotten what it was all about. It arose after the persecution under Diocletian, as the schism of Novatus arose, in Cyprian's day, after the persecution under Decius. It began with the same question, What shall be done with those who, in terror of death, denied the faith? And there were two answers, as before: the answer of charity and the answer of severity. The followers of Donatus were on the side of severity, and they went out of the Church, as the followers of Novatus had done, and started a Christian society of their own. The new church claimed to be the true church. It had its own bishops, whom it set up in city after city against the bishops already in control. There were two kinds of Christians, Catholics and Donatists. And they began to fight.

The Catholic Christians, as they were called who belonged to the old church, appealed to the emperor. And Constantine, who was then on the imperial throne, sent soldiers to Africa, where the Donatists were in the greatest numbers, to put them down. But this only made bad matters worse. The Donatists, who had rebelled against the Church, now rebelled against the State. They became the enemies of the established order. Some of them went about in gangs with clubs, and broke into Catholic churches, and beat the Catholic clergy.

They were good men, too, many of these Donatists. They fought for freedom of conscience. They protested against the endeavor of the State to make them change their religion by sending soldiers against them; and against the endeavor of the Church to make them submit to rules which they considered wrong.

All wrongs and rights, however, were now confused in the long contention. It was impossible even to discuss the differences in any fair and friendly spirit. Augustine tried it. There was a great debate at Carthage, with Augustine on one side and a Donatist on the other, but it came to nothing. It came, indeed, to worse than nothing, for Augustine in his earnestness for the order and strength of the Church was led to take Christ's words out of the parable where He said, " Compel them to come in," and to apply them to all who were in a state of schism. Compel them to come in. Persuade them, argue with them, and thus, if possible, convert them; but if you cannot convert them, compel them. Send soldiers after them, beat them, burn their churches, drag them in. It was said in a moment of deep discouragement and indignation, but it was never forgotten. It was applied to people in heresy and schism for hundreds of cruel years.

The heresy of Pelagius first appeared in public in a letter which he wrote to a young Roman lady who had resolved to forsake the world and thenceforth to live a single life of prayer and fasting. Many of her friends sent letters of congratulation. Jerome was particularly enthusiastic. Pelagius, however, was not so sure about it. The world, he said, is indeed a bad world, but not so hopelessly bad. It is not necessary to go out of it in order to live a righteous life: nor does it greatly matter, so far as holiness is concerned, whether one is married or unmarried.

The letter came to the attention of Augustine, and he condemned the opinion of Pelagius. Taking his own experience of evil in his early life, and confirming it with sentences from the writings of St.

Paul, he maintained that human nature is bad completely. Man is, by nature, depraved totally, and comes into the world in sin, the child of the devil; so that even a helpless infant, dying before he has done either right or wrong, must go into everlasting punishment for the sin which is born in him; unless he has been born again in baptism. Nothing that we can do, Augustine said, can save us, no works of goodness, no life of righteousness: we must be saved by the act of God. And God, he added, saves us, not because we deserve it, but because of His own pleasure. Some He has eternally predestined to be saved, others to be lost. Our hope is not in our own merits, but in His mercy; and our help is in the grace of God, gained for us by the death of Jesus Christ, and given to us in the sacraments of the Church.

The effect of this teaching was to increase the importance of the Church. The

world was represented as in the days of
Noah, wholly bad and under a destroying
flood. The Church was like the ark.
Whoever would be saved must get into
it, through the door of baptism. Outside
were angry waters, and howling winds,
and sure destruction.

So it seemed to Augustine, and the age
in which he lived illustrated it. Year by
years rose the unescapable flood of the barbarian invasion. Goths, Huns, and Vandals threatened the empire. They came
over the ancient boundaries of the Danube and the Rhine. They devastated
cities, and laid waste great tracts of culti-
vated country. And wherever they came,
they stayed. They took possession.

Finally, in 410, Alaric the Goth sacked
Rome. The Romans had believed, concerning Rome, as the Jews believed concerning
Jerusalem, that it could not be taken. It
had so long ruled the world, that it seemed
a part of the nature of things, like the ever-

lasting sun. But the soldiers of Alaric conquered it. The ancient city was given over to sword and flame. Amidst a thousand other acts of terror, the Goths broke into the house of Marcella, and so beat her that she died in a few days.

Only the Roman emperor seemed unmoved by this tremendous calamity. He was in a safe retreat at Ravenna when the news came. It is remembered of the emperor Honorius that there were only two matters in which he was ever known to show the slightest interest: one was the safety of his own imperial person, the others was the raising of hens, in which he was very successful. His favorite hen was named Rome. When they came, then, crying, "Your Majesty, Rome has perished!" he said, "Why, only an hour ago she was feeding out of my hand!" And when they told him that it was the capital of the world which had been destroyed, he was much relieved.

The Goths under Alaric spread over Italy. After them came the Vandals under Genseric, and invaded Roman Africa. Augustine saw them coming, a long way off. He saw that the catastrophe long dreaded had at last arrived. The Roman Empire had fallen. The old power which governed the world had met defeat. The old cities had new inhabitants. Rome had fallen, and the Roman age had come to a tragic end.

In the midst of this situation, the news of the march of the barbarians coming daily to his ears, Augustine wrote his great book, the "City of God." The city of Rome, he said, has indeed perished, but there is another city, the Church of Christ, eternal in the heavens.

Augustine was now an old man, and ill. And the Vandals were storming the walls of Hippo. He could hear the cries of battle from his sick-bed. "I have but one prayer to God amid these calamities,"

he said, " either that He would set this
city free from the enemy, or if not, that
He would make His servants strong to
bear His will, or at least that He would
take me to Himself from the world."
The end of the prayer was answered.
Augustine died. The city, deserted by its
inhabitants, was burnt by the Vandals to
the ground.

ST. JOHN AND ST. BENEDICT

From the picture by Perugino in the monastery of Santa
Maria Maddalena, Florence

BENEDICT

480-543

WHEN it was reported in Rome that a man was living in a cave in a wild gorge by the river Anio, forty miles away, people. were interested but not surprised. It was not at that time an uncommon thing to live in a cave.

The monastic life, whose joys Jerome had preached to the ladies of Roman society, had by this time attracted great numbers of people, in the West as in the East. This was due in part to two exceedingly popular books which everybody read: the "Life of St. Anthony," by Athanasius, and the "Life of St. Martin," by Sulpicius Severus. The patience and devotion of Anthony in Egypt were equalled, if not surpassed, by the spiritual virtues and adventures of Martin in France.

It was Martin who, in his youth, a cavalryman in the army of the emperor Julian, saw a shivering beggar by the roadside, and cutting his military cloak in two flung half over the beggar's back, and that night in vision saw the Lord in heaven wearing the garment which he had thus given in compassion. It was Martin to whom once appeared a vision of the Lord in shining apparel, with a chariot of fire, and invited the saint to ride with Him to the gates of Paradise; and Martin, looking attentively at Him, said, " Where are the marks of the nails? " There were no marks of the nails, and the vision, which was a trick of the devil, vanished in a cloud of evil smoke.

The marks of the nails were evident in all the life of Martin, who put himself to much privation, gave his days and nights to prayer, went about his great

pagan diocese on foot, braved a savage
emperor who had behaved unjustly, and
a whole community of wild heathen whose
sacred tree he cut down with his own
ax, and alike by his courage and his
gentleness appealed to the imagination of
earnest youth.

St. Anthony and St. Martin, then, were
the heroes of the devout life of the fifth
century. The man in the cave knew by
heart the books which told about them.

And, as another and still stronger argument for the forsaking of the world, was the
condition of the world itself. All things
were in confusion. Alaric the Goth and
Genseric the Vandal were followed by
Attila the Hun, and by a thousand other
lesser captains. The Lombards were
settling in the north of Italy. The Franks
were taking France. The old laws were
no longer a protection, the old customs
were giving place to new, the wealthy
and educated Latins were thrust out of

their pleasant houses and these conquerors, uneducated, only partially civilized, speaking strange languages, took possession. The Goths, indeed, had become Christians; but their Christianity was of the Arian kind. And when the Franks, under their king Clovis, were converted and became Catholic Christians, the Franks and the Goths fell to fighting, and the miseries of the times were multiplied. No peaceful citizen could be sure when he went to bed at night that his house would not be burned down before morning. Under these circumstances, even a cave in a dark gorge, while it might not be very comfortable, had at least the advantage of being safe.

So thought Benedict when he hid himself beside the river Anio. He belonged to a noble family in Rome, and spent his youth there. And when he had had enough, and more than enough, of the hard world, he put it all behind him, and found peace and the presence of God in his cave. He had a friend who every day lowered over the face of the cliff to the mouth of the cave a little basket of bread. A bell tied to the basket informed the hermit that his dinner was approaching.

The reports which were carried about by neighboring shepherds concerning the holiness of the man in the cave caused the monks of a monastery in that region to invite him to be their abbot. "You don't want me for your abbot," said Benedict, when they appeared at the mouth of the cave with their request. "You don't know what sort of man I am. You would not be willing to live according to my rule." But the monks were full of enthusiasm at the idea of a holy abbot and a better life, and they insisted till Benedict consented. So he took command, and at the end of the first week they tried to poison him.

This experience disclosed the fact that the monastic life needed reforming. A hundred other houses of religion were like the abbey whose monks had found the discipline of Benedict too hard. Men had gone into monasticism for a great number of reasons: because they were afraid of Franks and Goths, because they had failed in business or in love, because they did not wish to work. And, having become monks, they were living pretty much as they pleased, some starving and some feasting; some saying their prayers, some breaking the Commandments. There was no order, or regularity, or common discipline. There was no accepted rule.

When Benedict returned to his cave beside the Anio, his former solitude had become impossible. Good people were greatly interested in the abbot who was so strict that his monks had put poison in his cup. Disciples gathered about him. Noble Roman families sent their sons to him to be instructed in religion. Presently, on the wild hills in the neighbor-

hood of Benedict's cave were twelve
groups of men in twelve monastic houses,
living according to his regulations.

But the world was still too near, and the
monks sought a more secure retreat. To
the south was a range of mountains, and
on the summit of one of them, called
Monte Cassino, they found a little temple
with an altar dedicated to Apollo, standing
in a grove. There were still a few country people who came to offer their sacri-
fices in the old way. It was one of many
hidden places, among the woods and in
the high hills, where the Roman gods
were still remembered. These simple people Benedict converted. Their temple to
Apollo he destroyed, and on its site he
began the building of a monastery, which
became the most famous and influential in
all Europe.

For the monks of Monte Cassino, Benedict wrote a rule of life, which was so
good that all other monks adopted it.

Even to-day, wherever there is a monastery, the conduct of its life is still governed by St. Benedict.

He found the monks, following the example of the East, devoting themselves to pain and prayer, living their own religious life for the good of their own souls. Benedict brought them back to save the world which they had abandoned. He stopped the old tortures. He forsook all that starving and beating of the body which good men had undertaken in the deserts of the Nile in the hope of improving their souls. For pain he substituted work. The fare of the monks was to be plain and frugal, but not to the extent of hardships. Their work was to be, in part in the field, cultivating the soil, and in part in the cloister, reading, and studying, and teaching.

The influence of these provisions was far-reaching and of vast importance.

The Latins had despised all labor of

the hands. They had had slaves to do that, and it was associated with slavery. It was accounted a disgrace for a free man to work. Benedict and his monks put a stop to that mischievous prejudice. Men saw these gentlemen and saints planting their fields, mowing their grain, gathering their fruit. The sight dignified all the humble life of the farm. The first thing which the monks did when they established a monastery in a wild place was to clear the land, and they got their barbarian neighbors to follow their example.

As for the labor of the mind, the Goths and Franks were unaccustomed to it. When they came on their fierce invasions they brought no books, and those which they found they could not read. For many years they were too busy fighting, and then settling, making themselves the new masters of the old empire, to pay attention to learning. The reading monks did that.

They preserved the ancient Latin books. They saved Virgil and Horace and Cicero, and all the Latin classics from destruction. They were the teachers of the new generations.

Thus, when Benedict wrote in his rule, " Idleness is the enemy of the soul; and therefore the brethren ought to employ themselves at certain times in the work of the hands, and again at certain times in divine reading," the words were such as to exercise an influence for the good of the world greater than that of all the books which had been written since the New Testament.

It is the province and privilege of the men who come first to clear the way and build foundations. Thus Cyprian was the pioneer of the Church: he first brought the Christian society into its place of future importance in the Christian religion. Athanasius was the pioneer of the creed: he first insisted on the essential

importance of an accurate statement of
the faith. Ambrose and Chrysostom were
splendid examples of the leadership of
religion against unrighteousness. Jerome
gave Western Christendom the Bible in
its own language. Augustine contributed
a system of theology, partly true and
partly untrue, which, for good and evil,
governed the minds of men during the suc-
ceeding centuries. Benedict set in order
that monastic life which carried religion
and civilization through the confusion of
the fall of the Roman Empire.

Beside the monastery in which Benedict
lived his good life, his devout sister,
Scholastica had a holy house, filled with
praying and working women. The rules
which they had made permitted the
brother and sister to see each other only
once a year. So Benedict came, one time,
in his old age, to visit Scholastica, and
when he rose to go, she begged him to
stay longer, and talk of heavenly things.

And when he persisted, feeling that he had already stayed his time, the sky, the monks said, became black with a great storm, and the rain fell so that he could not go. That was their last visit.

GREGORY THE GREAT

From the painting by Justus van Ghent, Barberini Palace, Rome

GREGORY THE GREAT
540-604

A ROMAN senator, rich and of an ancient family, was so attracted by the Order of St. Benedict that he built six monasteries in Rome; and then a seventh, in which he went to live himself, and became its abbot. His name was Gregory, surnamed "the Great."

One day as the abbot walked about the streets, he saw that there were slaves for sale.

There were always slaves for sale in Rome. Some were men who had got so deep in debt that they could not get out, and, having sold all else which they possessed, at last sold themselves. But most of them were captives from the wars. All the borders of the Roman Empire blazed with war. Even after the barbarians came and destroyed the old empire, still they fought among themselves. And after every battle, the victors, whether they were Romans or Goths or Franks, gathered up a great company of prisoners and sold them in the nearest market. It was better than the former custom of putting them all to death. And it was better sometimes than the modern custom of putting them in military jails without sufficient food or shelter.

The consequence was that the slave trade was a flourishing business in Rome, and Gregory, kind-hearted and large-minded though he was, never thought of trying to stop it.

A new lot of captives had come that day, sent down from Britain. They were of the race called Angles, from whom England got its first name of Angle-land. They came from that western part of Yorkshire which was then called Deira. Their yellow hair and fair skin pleased the eyes of

Gregory, and he stopped to question them. "Whence do you come?" he said. "We are Angles," they replied, "from the kingdom of Deira. "God be gracious to you, my children," said the abbot. "You are Angles? You are as fair as angels. You should be Christians. I will go myself to your land of Deira, and save your people *de ira*—from the ire, from the wrath,— of God."

Gregory did not go to England, as he hoped, because he was detained in Rome. The pope died, and all the people demanded Gregory, as the Christians of Carthage had called for Cyprian, and the Christians of Milan for Ambrose. The desire was unanimous. The people wanted him, the clergy wanted him, the senate wanted him. He wrote a letter to the emperor begging him to forbid the election, but somebody took the letter and never sent it. There was no escape. So Gregory became the pope of Rome.

One time, just before Jerome went to Rome to begin his classes in the house of Marcella, there were two men, each of whom greatly desired to be bishop, and their followers had such a battle in the Church of Sta. Maria Maggiore that, when it was over, a hundred and thirty-seven dead bodies lay upon the floor. It shows not only what a fierce and disorderly time it was, but how much men prized the office. Gregory, indeed, did not desire it, but that was because he did not care for wealth or power.

The pope of Rome was bishop of the greatest city in the world. The Vandals had ruined Carthage; Constantinople and Alexandria were far away. Rome had no rival. It is true that the emperor had ceased to live there; but his departure had increased the importance of the bishop, for he was now the leading citizen. He was the most prominent and influential Christian in the Western Church. The invading barbarians cared little for the old empire, but they had some respect for the Christian religion. Gradually, by the good services of missionaries, many of them from the monasteries of St. Benedict, it became their religion. It was the only living survivor of the old world which they had destroyed. Whatever of ancient custom and culture and learning had remained, was in the Church. The Church was the sole representative in all Europe of that departed civilization which had built the great cities, made the enduring roads, carved the statues, and written the books. And the leader and spokesman of the Church was the bishop of Rome.

Moreover, just about the time when Gregory was questioning the Angle slaves, there was born in Arabia a man who was to change the whole course of the history of the Christian East. Out of Mecca came Mohammed. To the conquest of the west of Christendom by the Goths and Vandals, was added the conquest of the East by the Mohammedans. But the Mohammedans did not become Christians like the Goths. They came in the strength of their own religion, hating the religion of the Christains, and they took possession of almost the whole of the Eastern empire. They captured Jerusalem. They made themselves masters of the Holy Land. They took Alexandria. They were long delayed in taking Constantinople, but they deprived it of its ancient power. Thus the successors of Gregory became, not only the greatest bishops in the West, but the greatest in the world.

This was the office which prevented Gregory from going to England.

A great slab of stone in the Forum at Rome still shows the carved picture of the emperor Trajan distributing food to widows and orphans. This was the Trajan to whom Pliny wrote in 112 to ask what should be done to stop the dangerous growth of the Christians. One day, as Pope Gregory passed that way, he stopped in front of the stone picture and looked at it with great appreciation. It seemed to him a pleasant memorial of ancient times and of a good and friendly man. That day, at prayer, he ventured to pray for Trajan, that he might be pardoned for his paganism, and admitted into the Christian heaven. And in a dream the Lord appeared to the devout pope. "Gregory," he said, "you have prayed for the pardon of a pagan, and I have granted your petition; but do not do it again." The story shows how the theology of Augustine had taken hold of the minds of men, who thus found it possible to believe that all the heathens, good and bad, were lost. But it reveals also the fellowship of Gregory with anybody who had tried to help his neighbors.

Gregory's ministry was spent in such good deeds. He took a great and useful

part in all the life about him: dealt with
Arians, who were still troubling Italy, and
with Donatists, who were still troubling
Africa; disciplined idle and unworthy
monks and ministers; attended to the needs
of the poor and the sick; and gave his
farmer careful directions about the working of his farm. He interested himself in
the music of the Church, and introduced a
way of chanting which bears his name,
and is still in general use. He added a
prayer to that Communion Service which
is called the Mass, and thereby completed
it in the form in which it is said to-day.
The Latin of that service, as it is used in
every Roman Catholic church, is substan-
tially as it came from the hands of Gregory.

Nothing, however, that Gregory did
was of so much importance to us as his
sending of a board of missionaries to convert the English.

The Christian Church had been planted

in Britain so early in history that nobody
knows when or by whom: probably by
Christian soldiers in Roman legions.
There it was, however, in that land which
the Romans had conquered, and to which
many wealthy Romans loved to go in the
cool summer. Constantine had started
from York on that eventful march which
made him the first Christian emperor.
And when, presently, he called a conference of bishops to consider the case of the
Donatists, three of the bishops came from
Britain.

Then the Angles and Saxons invaded
Britain. The Roman legions had been
called home to defend Rome, and the
Britons, who had depended on their arms,
were without defense. They were driven
out of their fair country, from their pleasant cities and their churches, into the
mountains of Wales. The pagan invaders
changed Britain into England. Between
the Christian Britons and their Christian

brethren on the continent of Europe was
thrust this wedge of English heathenism.

Gregory remembered the Angle slaves.
Out of one of the Benedictine monasteries
which he had built, he chose a man named
Augustine, and sent him with a band of
forty monks to England. The missionaries to the English pagans went up
through France; and, whenever they
stopped to spend the night, such terrifying
tales were told them of the fierce ways of
the barbarous English, that they stopped,
and sent a letter back to Gregory, asking
to be relieved from such a dangerous mission. But Gregory urged them on.

Thus in 597,—a date to be remembered,
—they crossed the channel, and set their
feet upon the soil of heathen England. But
there were friends to meet them. Bertha,
the Queen of Ethelbert of Kent, was already a Christian, being a daughter of the
King of the Franks, who had his throne at
Paris. She had kept her religion in the

midst of the paganism of the new country, and had caused to be rebuilt, near Canterbury, where she lived, a little ruined church. This she dedicated to the brave memory of St. Martin, who had contended so faithfully with the pagans of his neighborhood, and out to little St. Martin's she was wont to go to say her Christian prayers.

Ethelbert, accordingly, knew who the Christians were; though he knew so little about them that he preferred to meet the missionaries in the open air, lest they should bewitch him with some spell. He sat, therefore, under a tree, and watched Augustine and his men as they approached, the forty of them in procession, carrying a banner, and singing a litany to the music which they had been taught by Gregory. The king listened gravely as Augustine preached the religion of Christ, and promised to consider the matter carefully. Meanwhile the missionaries were given freedom to teach, and houses in Canterbury in which to live, and, pretty soon, St. Martin's church in which to worship God.

The fact that the missionaries came from Rome, that distant and renowned capital of the world, emphasized their message; and it was further confirmed by their holy living. Thus one heathen Englishman after another was converted; presently, the king himself; and after the king, following his good example, ten thousand of his subjects in one day.

Then Augustine was made a bishop,— the first bishop of the English. Ethelbert gave him his own palace; and a ruined British church beside it became the beginning of the Cathedral of Canterbury. The Christian religion was thus introduced among our ancestors, the English.

Gregory sent to Augustine a letter of wise advice. Do not destroy the temples of the English gods, he said; change them

into Christian churches. Do not forbid
the harmless customs which have been
associated with the old religion; consecrate
them, like the churches, to Christian uses.
Let them revere the saints where they have
worshiped idols. Thus, he said, " having
some outward joys continued to them, they
may more easily accept the true inward
joys. For assuredly it is impossible to cut
away all things at once from minds hard-
ened by evil custom; just as the man who
strives to reach the summit of perfection,
climbs by steps and paces, not by leaps
and bounds."

It was in accordance with this sensible
advice that the missionaries called the festival of Christ's resurrection " Easter,"
from Eostre, the English goddess of the
spring. The Christmas season they called
" Yule-tide," from an English god of the
winter; and they still brought in the yule
log from the woods, and hung the mistle-
toe upon the walls, as the ancestors of the

English had done in the long-gone days before ever an Englishman had heard of Christ or had set his foot in England.

Thus Tuesday kept the old name of Tuesco, the god of war; and Wednesday, of Woden, the father of the gods; and Thursday, of Thor, the god of thunder; and Friday, of Frigg, the goddess of love; by the courtesy of Gregory the Great.

COLUMBA

From the statue by Gutzon Borglum, Cathedral of
St. John the Divine, New York

COLUMBA

521-597

WHEN the news spread through the mountains of Wales and along the coasts of Cornwall that Roman Catholics had come to convert the heathen English, the British Christians sent messengers to meet them. They held a conference together under an oak beside the river Severn.

The Britons looked upon their Roman brethren as Robinson Crusoe looked upon the English sailors who landed on his island. They had been cut off from the rest of the civilized world for a hundred and fifty years. Much of that time had been spent in hard fighting, and most of the fighting had ended in defeat. They had been driven from their ancient cities into the wild hills. Stories were still told of the brave battles which their splen-

did heroes, the Knights of the Round
Table, had fought against the invading
Angles. But the book in which the stories
are collected is called "The Death of
Arthur." The knights are vanquished at
the end, and the king is killed.

Two possessions the Britons had brought
down through the long tragedy of the war,
their language and their religion.

They still spoke that Celtic speech in
which their ancestors had shouted war
cries against Julius Cæsar, and which their
descendants speak to this day in Wales.

And they still kept the Christian faith,
and prayed the Christian prayers. It is
true that they had not attempted to convert the English, but that was because
the fighting had been so fierce, and their
sufferings so great. One of them, however, a lad named Patrick, had been captured by Irish pirates in 411, the year
after the withdrawal of the Roman legions,
and had introduced the Christian religion

into Ireland. Other missionaries of their race, from Ireland, had introduced it into Scotland. There were many British bishops. In a monastery at Bangor lived as many as two thousand monks, though not one of them had ever heard of Benedict or his famous Rule. One Briton, the good heretic Pelagius, had made such a stir, even in Rome, that Augustine of Carthage had heard of it in Africa.

Thus the Britons who met Augustine of Canterbury represented the Christianity, not only of Wales and Cornwall, but of Ireland and of Scotland. Augustine, however, fresh from Rome, regarded them with that curiosity and superiority with which people from the city sometimes regard the inhabitants of the backwoods. He asked them various questions and discovered various differences which had naturally arisen in consequence of their long separation from the rest of the Church. The most serious of these differences was a mistake in the almanac. They had lost count of the date of Easter. Augustine required them to correct these errors. And they went back to consult their brethren in the matter.

On the whole, there was a disposition to yield these unimportant things and to agree to what the Romans asked. The chief obstacle was the way in which the Romans asked it. Their manner was exceedingly superior and uncivil. As the Britons were on their way to a second conference, they asked the counsel of a holy hermit. He said, " Watch Augustine. If, when you approach, he rises to meet you, like a gentleman, do as he requests. If he remains seated, beware how you submit to his authority." So they came to the place of meeting, and there sat Augustine, and he continued sitting. Then they returned to their own place, and left the Romans to carry on their mission by themselves. And Augustine, having his residence at

Canterbury, went forward with the conversion of Kent; and presently Paulinus, taking up his residence at York, began the conversion of Northumbria.

Now the same year in which Augustine came to Kent saw the end of the long and useful life of Columba. He was the pioneer of the missions in the North, as Augustine and Paulinus were the pioneers of the missions in the South.

The stories of the early life of Columba show that he was very fond of praying, of reading, and of fighting.

His Irish name was Colum of the Kil; Kil meaning cell, or church. Ireland was already full of churches, and Colum was famous, all the country round, for the frequency and enthusiasm with which he visited them.

The first adventure which is remembered of him was about a book. Of course, in those days, whoever wanted a book must either buy, or borrow, or copy

one.   And in Ireland they were very expert
in the writing which preceded printing,
with illuminated initials and a peculiarly
intricate interlacing of lines to decorate
the pages. So Colum of the Kil copied
a gospel book which was the property of
his neighbor Finnian, sitting up nights
to do it after his day's work. But when
the copy was completed Finnian claimed
it as his own. Finnian said that "it was
to himself belonged the Son-book which
was written from his book." They referred the matter to King Dermot, and he
decided against Columba, saying, "To
every book belongs its Son-book, as to
every cow belongs its calf."

According to one account, it was this
unfair decision which led to the great fight
between Columba and the king, but another story refers this battle to the Feast
of Tara. The king lived at Tara, and
there he made a feast, and minstrels sang
to the music of their harps, and there was

much eating and more drinking, and by-
and-by the guests fell so merrily to fighting that one of them was killed. The
chief whose sword had fallen so heavily
on his neighbor's head fled from the vengeance of King Dermot to the protection
of Columba, who was already famous as
both a saint and a hero. But even there
the avenging king laid hands upon him,
and had his head. Then it was Columba's
turn for vengeance. He gathered together
all his kinsfolk, the clan of the northern
Neills, and they attacked the king. They
fought and Columba prayed. It was like
the cursing of Tara, when all the clergy
helped the chiefs who besieged the king
in his hall; they rang their bells, and
chanted psalms, and " fasted on him."
And he lost the battle.

Out of this wild Ireland, thus partly
Christian but partly savage, Columba took
his journey after these bloody doings, being
expelled, some say, for his share in them.

He set out in a little wicker boat, with a few companions. and they sailed and sailed. Once they were about to land upon an island, but when they looked back there was still a glimpse of Ireland on the far horizon, and they pushed forward. Thus they came at last to the island of Iona.

Iona is off the west coast of Scotland, south of Staffa which people visit to see the curious stone columns of Fingal's cave. It is a little island, not much more than three miles wide at its greatest width. There are ruins of an old cathedral, but not so old as the days of St. Columba; and there are stone crosses carved with the same complicated interlacing of lines which appears in the ancient Irish books. Only two things remain to recall the presence of the saint: one is the Gaelic language, akin to the Welsh of the old Britons, the other is the island itself, and particularly a little bay in the south whose beach is covered with shining pebbles, which the sun and the sea make to look like precious stones. There the little band of exiles landed.

They built upon the island some rude shelter for themselves, and a place in which to worship God. Then they set out upon a series of adventurous voyages to the mainland. The north of Scotland was inhabited by the Picts. Columba converted their king and the people followed his example. The south of Scotland was inhabited by the Scots. They had a new king, whom Columba blessed and crowned. The king's rude palace was at Scone, and some say that the king sat to be crowned upon the rough stone which the English, when they conquered Scotland, brought to London. Anyhow, there is the Stone of Scone in the coronation chair of England, to recall the fact that the first Christian king crowned in Great Britain was crowned by St. Columba.

Iona was the training place of all the missionaries who went on their wild adventurous journeys in the North. By-and-by, men from Iona founded a mission station on another little island off the east coast of England, and called it Lindisfarne, the Holy Island.

There is a glimpse of the labors of Columba in the story of another mission, where a Christian preacher brought the gospel to the Northumbrians. The king called a conference of his great men, and they all listened. And one said, "I have been faithful to the religion of our fathers and it has profited me nothing. The old gods have made me neither rich nor happy. I am willing to make trial of these new ones." And another said, "Our life is like the flight of a bird through our lighted hall. In comes the bird out of the dark, flies about a little while in the smoke and light of our fires and torches, and then goes out into the dark. Thus we come and go. If these strangers can tell us anything about these mysteries of birth and death, let us attend to their teaching." Thus converts were made. The tragedy and the mystery of life impelled men to seek a better explanation of the world than their own religion gave.

The heart of all this journeying and preaching was Columba. He was a great broad-chested, stout-armed person; "not a gentle hero," an old record says. He loved to drive his little boat into the middle of the fiercest storms. His voice was like the bellow of a bull of Bashan. He slept on the bare ground, and was contented with rough fare. He carried his corn on his own back to the mill, ground it, and brought it home again. He prayed and studied; and fought, too, when there was occasion. His people loved him.

One day, in his old age, he climbed a little hill and looked out over the humble buildings of his monastery, and the fields in which his monks were working, and blessed them all. As he came down and sat to rest himself beside the barn, the old white work-horse came and laid his head against his breast. He had been copying the Psalms, as at the beginning he had copied Finnian's Gospel. "They who seek the Lord," he wrote, "shall want no manner of thing that is good." It seemed a fitting place to stop. He laid down his pen. Late that night he went alone into the little church, and in the morning there he was found dead, kneeling before the altar.

In "Macbeth," when one asks, after the murder of the king, "Where is Duncan's body?" the reply is

"*Carried to Colme-Kill [Columba's Island],
The sacred storehouse of his predecessors,
And guardian of their bones.*"

In the little cemetery beside the church they buried kings, from Ireland, from Scotland, even from Norway, that in the Day of Judgment they might rise up in the good protecting company of St. Columba.

CHARLEMAGNE

742-814

THE story of the Knights of Arthur ends in defeat.

The king dreamed a strange and dreadful dream. It seemed to him that he was sitting in a chair, dressed in the richest cloth-of-gold that ever was made; and under him was "a hideous deep black water, and therein were all manner of serpents, and worms and wild beasts, foul and terrible," and suddenly the chair turned upside down, and he fell among the serpents, and "every beast took him by a limb." It is a picture of the fall of the Britons into the cruel power of their enemies the Angles.

The story of the Knights of Charlemagne is also a story of defeat.

The king has been fighting with the

CHARLEMAGNE

Saracens. Out of Arabia have come those wild soldiers of Mohammed to invade Europe. They are threatening both the religion and the civilization of the West. They have destroyed the Eastern empire, and are now proceeding to take the Western empire out of the hands of its barbarian conquerors. Their purpose is to make Arabia a world-power, such as Assyria and Chaldea, and Greece and Rome had been. They intend to annex Europe to Arabia, and to make Rome, as they had already made Jerusalem, subject to Mecca. The situation is like that in the days when Xerxes came with his Persians to the conquest of Greece, and was met by Leonidas at the Pass of Thermopolæ.

Thus the Saracens are met by Roland and Oliver at the Pass of Roncesvalles. And, as in the old time, there is a traitor. Ganelon, the false knight, shows a way by which the men who fight under the Crescent may have the advantage of the men who fight under the Cross. Charlemagne and the greater part of the army have gone on ahead, but Roland will not sound his horn to call them back. He will not ask for help. " Please God and His Holy Angels," he cries, " France shall not be so shamed through me; better death than such dishonor. The harder we strike, the better the emperor will love us." So they strike, till all the sides of the mountains are filled with the bodies of the slain. At last, the leaders themselves fall.

There is this difference, however, between the Death of Arthur and the Song of Roland: the defeat of Arthur is the end of the story, but the defeat of Roland is only an incident. Back comes Charlemagne and puts the Saracens to flight. It illustrates the contrast between the Britons, fighting their losing battles against the Angles, and their kinsmen the Franks, fighting their winning battles

against the Angles' kinsmen, the Saxons.
This was mainly due to the might of
Charlemagne.

The Franks, over whom Charlemagne
was king, were Christians. But their
Saxon neighbors, to the north and east, in
Germany, were heathen. Christian missionaries had, indeed, been busy, following the brave examples of Patrick and
Columba and Augustine, and tribe after
tribe had yielded to the new religion.
Boniface, for example, had come down
from England, from the church which
had been formed at last by the union of
the missions of Columba with the missions of Augustine, and had won the title
of "Apostle of Germany." But he had
died a martyr, the pagan Frisians attacking him in his tent and putting him to
death. The Saxons were still unconverted.

High among the Saxon mountains, in
the forests of the Teutoberg, stood a tall,
mysterious column called the Irminsul.

It was the supreme idol of the Saxons. It looked down over the valleys into which, in the days of Augustine, the Saxons had enticed the legions under Varus, and had destroyed them. The Saxons prayed to it before they went to war. It represented the great god of Saxon Good Luck.

Of course, the Franks and Saxons fought continually. That was then the fashion among neighbors. The Saxons made their forays into the Frankish lands, and stole cattle and burned villages, and the Franks returned their visits. But more and more, as the Franks increased in civilization and in their knowledge of religion, the war between these tribes became a war between the reign of law and the reign of disorder, between learning and ignorance, and between Christianity and paganism. It was a new mission. Boniface had gone with the gospel, helped and defended only by his good life; and when at last the savage Frisians came howling about his tent, he would not permit any of his companions to strike a blow against them. Charlemagne came with the sword.

The first thing which he did was to destroy the Irminsul. Down came the sacred column crashing to the ground, and it seemed, for the moment, as if the religion and the might of the Saxons had fallen with it. But fighting the Saxons was like fighting a forest fire. While Charlemagne was putting out the flames of war in one place, they were breaking out more furiously than ever somewhere else. Every time he won a battle, he gathered his prisoners together, the vanquished chiefs and the subdued people, and marched them down into the nearest river and had them all baptized, every man of them. It was a queer kind of mission; and these converts often went back to paganism again when Charlemagne's back was turned, as might have been expected. But there were priests and bishops who went in among the people, dismayed as they were by the failure of their old gods to protect them, and taught them more effectively the truths to which the sword had so forcibly called their attention.

Thus Charlemagne became the master of all the tribes of Europe. All those various companies of barbarians who had broken down the old empire and settled among the ruins, and the wilder tribes who still lived, like the Saxons, in their native forests, were forced by his strong hand into obedience to a single government. He had the mind and the ambition of Alexander and of Cæsar, and belongs with them among the masters of the world.

So far did the great sound of his name go, that one time there came to him an embassy from the distant East, from Bagdad, sent by Harun-al-Raschid, out of the Arabian Nights; to see his court, as the Queen of Sheba came to see the glory of Solomon.

The eyes of the ambassadors of Harun-al-Raschid were probably attracted most by the armor of the knights and the ranks of the soldiers, and the stories which they told on their return were mostly about Roland and Oliver. But the most significant persons at the court of Charlemagne were schoolmasters and clergymen.

There had come down from England, from a school at York, a wise man named Alcuin. And when his errand was accomplished, and he was about to return, Charlemagne detained him. " Stay here," he said, " and teach us."

They needed him, that was plain enough. The great men were soldiers, who knew much about war but nothing about books. They were aware in a dim way that a race had preceded them in those lands who, though they had finally been conquered, had excelled their conquerors in art and architecture, in science and letters, in law and order. They had about them continual reminders of that old civilization, in the remains of Latin roads and buildings. They felt themselves in the neighborhood of a buried treasure to which the clue was lost. In Alcuin, they found the man who had the clue. He knew the old history, and was acquainted with the old art, and was able to read the old books. They became his pupils, beginning with the emperor himself. And some of those whom Alcuin taught established other schools, which grew in years to great universities.

These schoolmasters were clergymen. Many of them were monks of the Order of St. Benedict, and all looked to the Italy of Benedict and Gregory, as the Jews in the old time in exile when they said their prayers looked toward Jerusalem. There dwelt the bishop who was the head of all things religious as the emperor was the head of all things political. To the clergymen of the court of Charlemagne there were two great powers in the world: the power of the sword, which was held by Charlemagne, and was possessed by him as the master of the new empire of Franks and Saxons and Goths, builded on the ruins of the old; and the power of the spirit, which, as represented by the Church, and by the pope as the ruler of the Church, was bringing among these new masters of the world the civilization and the religion of the past.

But the pope was beset by enemies: by the Lombards, who had invaded Italy and seized lands there and who, though Christians, were of the Arian kind; by the Greeks, who still had colonies in Italy, and whose allegiance, like that of the pope himself, was to the emperor whose throne was at Constantinople. He was still, in law, the emperor of Rome. Charlemagne came to the assistance of the pope.

On Christmas Day, in the year 800, the pope at that time being Leo III., Charlemagne was in Rome, and attended the service in St. Peter's Church. Suddenly, as he knelt before the altar, the pope placed upon his head a golden crown, and pronounced him emperor of Rome.

It meant that the new time had finally come. It completed the barbarian conquest. It announced that the old imperial line was set aside, that the West was independent of the East, and that the true successor of the ancient emperors was Charlemagne the Frank. It was the beginning of a new order of things, the Holy Roman Empire.

In this Holy Roman Empire Charlemagne was supreme. He ruled the Church as he ruled the State. He built churches and monasteries; he sent missionaries and appointed bishops. He fulfilled the proud words of Constantius, who said, " What I wish is a canon of the Church, and what I believe is an article of the creed." But happily, he was as wise as he was strong, a good man, honestly intent on the welfare of his people. So he died, full of years and honors, a true successor, not in name only, but in character and power, of the great emperors, and, like them, not emperor only, but Pontifex Maximus also.

Thus was played the first act in that great contention between the emperor and the pope for mastery, which is the tragedy of the Middle Ages. The emperor was supreme. The hero of the next act was Hildebrand.

HILDEBRAND
1020-1085

A NEW pope was on his way to Rome. He had been duly appointed by the emperor, according to the custom; and in his robes of office, with a splendid retinue about him, he was taking his great journey. But on the road he was met by a young monk. The monk said, "Father, you are not the pope of Rome. You have been appointed by the emperor, but the pope must be elected by the Church."

Thereupon the new pope put off his robes of office, dismissed his retinue of attendant knights and bishops, and entered Rome dressed in the gown of a pilgrim, with bare feet. There he was greeted with enthusiasm by the clergy and the people and they elected him to be their pope, according to the ancient manner.

The monk who gave the pope this good advice was Hildebrand.

Hildebrand's father was a carpenter, but he had an uncle who was a Roman abbot. With his uncle he studied, and when one of his teachers in the abbey was made pope, Hildebrand became his chaplain. But the popes of that period were short-lived. Some of them died of sickness, some of them died of poison, some of them displeased the emperor and were removed by him. Hildebrand's teacher was removed by the emperor. Then the chaplain retired to the great monastery at Cluny. And there he was when he advised the new pope to wait till he was elected by the Church.

It is plain that Hildebrand, though he was living in a cloister, was attentive to the affairs of the great world. Many good men at that time, finding the world bad, turned their backs upon it, and tried to forget it, except when they said their prayers. Hildebrand determined to change it. Great bishops came to Cluny as they passed that way, and great nobles with them. And they all looked pretty much alike. The bishops were rich and powerful, with vast estates, fond of hunting, fond of eating and drinking, and neglectful of their duties. They were appointed to their places by kings and princes, and spent much of their time in courts and palaces, and the clergy under them, having such examples set for them to follow, and nobody to keep them in order, fell into temptation. They cared for money and the comforts of life, rather than for religion.

Hildebrand saw that the situation needed a strong hand.

When the new pope went to Rome in pilgrim's dress, Hildebrand went with him. He became his chief adviser. He advised him to assert himself. He urged him to gather conferences of bishops for the reformation of abuses, and to do it without asking the permission of princes. The pope died, and the Roman people desired that Hildebrand should succeed him. He preferred to be the power behind the pope. He secured the appointment of Victor; and after Victor, of Stephen; and after Stephen, of Nicholas; and after Nicholas, of Alexander. Thus for twenty-five years, he was the real pope.

Finally, after the death of Alexander, the whole city insisted that he should be pope, not only in power, but in name. They demanded Hildebrand, as the people in the old days had demanded Cyprian, and Ambrose, and Gregory. It was the custom for one who was elected pope to take a new name in honor of his new office. Hildebrand remembered his old schoolmaster, Gregory VI., whom he had served as chaplain, and became Gregory VII.

Now, after long preparation, he was ready to meet the evils of the world with his own strong hand.

His plan was to make the Church the ruler of the world. He took up that great fight against the court which Chrysostom, in his time, had lost, and Ambrose had won.

First, he made the clergy into soldiers of a spiritual army. He separated them from the world. This he did by forbidding them to marry. They were living comfortably with their wives and children, having their interests partly in the work of the Church, and partly in their domestic cares and pleasures. They were not only priests, but husbands and fathers and citizens. Hildebrand determined that they should be interested in nothing but the Church. He broke up their families, and placed them, like soldiers, under the command of their superiors. This he was able to do partly because so many of the careless clergy were unpopular among their people, and partly because the monks had taught by word and by example that the unmarried life is most pleasing to God. The pope encouraged parishes to drive the married ministers out of the churches.

Then, having made the priests into a church army, he separated their offices from the influences of the world by forbidding the investiture of bishops. Investiture was the act by which a prince permitted a bishop to take possession of the lands and property which belonged to his diocese. The theory was that the prince owned all the land, and that when the holder of an estate died it came back into the prince's treasury until he was pleased to give it away again. Thus the new bishop came humbly to the prince or the king and received certain symbols of his right to own the church's property under this permission. Indeed, the symbols,—being the ring which denoted the bishop's marriage to the Church, and the pastoral staff which denoted his rule as a shepherd over his people,—appeared to carry with them, not only the right to hold the property of the Church, but the right to exercise the sacred office itself. That, in fact, was the effect of it. It made it possible for kings and princes to appoint bishops, and for rich laymen to appoint ministers of parishes, as they pleased. Hildebrand forbade investiture. He called a council in Rome which decreed that any clergyman who accepted an investiture should be put out of his office, and that any layman who gave an investiture should be put out of the Church.

This forbidding of investiture affected every bishop, as the forbidding of marriage had affected every priest. The next step was to increase the power of the pope. The priests having been made soldiers, and the bishops generals, the pope must be commander-in-chief. The pope, said Hildebrand, is the universal bishop. He may depose other bishops, if he will. He alone may make laws for the Church. He is to crown all kings and emperors, and, if they misbehave, depose them. He may absolve subjects from their allegiance. He is the supreme head of all government, the king of kings and lord of lords, the ruler of the world.

Some of these claims had been made before. Gradually, through the confused centuries when the old empire was being broken down and the new empire was being builded on its ruins, the position of the bishop of the greatest city of the world had become more and more important. Hildebrand took these theories and put them into action. The one man, by the might of his strong will and the power of his blameless life, confronted the whole amazed and angry society about him, declared with a definiteness which could not be mistaken that he was the master of all kingdoms and all churches, and proceeded to act upon the declaration.

Thus Hildebrand came into collision with the emperor.

Henry IV., as emperor of Germany, was the greatest sovereign in Europe. He was the successor, under the new conditions, of the old emperors of Rome. He was now twenty-five years of age, a careless prince, following his own pleasures and misgoverning the empire. Already, some of his subjects had appealed to the pope to make him amend his ways. The forbidding of investiture was met by him as the cutting off of patronage is met by professional politicians. It was an advantage to him to give away the great places of the Church, and he proposed to continue to do it. He attacked the pope.

He got his bishops together and they declared Hildebrand deposed. The emperor called him a false monk. He threatened to put another bishop in his place.

Thus they cursed each other, the emperor and the pope; but the pope's curses were the more effective. The unpopularity of the emperor weakened his position. When the pope declared him excommunicated and deposed, and thus made rebellion against him a religious duty, the princes of the empire found the opportunity which they desired. They gladly accepted the services of this new ally in their contention against the emperor whose follies had thrown the empire into disorder. Finding, accordingly, that both the princes and the clergy, and with them the people, were against him, Henry submitted to the pope's demands.

"You must come to me," the pope said, " and ask pardon for your offenses, and promise to do better. Otherwise, you shall be emperor no longer." And the emperor came.

It was in the midst of winter, and the pope was at Canossa, a castle in the heights of the Apennines. There the emperor came, with his wife and child and a few attendants, bringing his crown in his hand. For three days, Hildebrand kept him waiting outside his door, in the cold court of the castle, barefooted and in the woolen shirt of a penitent. Then he admitted him; and the great king, the ruler of the empire, the successor of Charlemagne, bareheaded and barefooted, prostrated himself with tears before the pope.

This was the second act in the long tragedy of the Middle Ages. The pope was now supreme over the emperor.

Even thus, Henry gained only a half pardon. He was told that he must be put on trial, with Hildebrand for judge; and if he was acquitted he must promise to be faithfully obedient to the pope.

The effect of all this on Henry was most unexpected. The second act of the tragedy seemed ended, when suddenly the situation was reversed. Henry went away from that humiliation a new man. As he descended the long mountain in the bitter cold, his heart was hot within him. He put the follies of his youth behind him. For the first time, he was a king in earnest. He gathered troops about him. He defied the nobles who were in rebellion. He invaded Italy. He besieged Rome. He took the city. Hildebrand held only the Castle of St. Angelo against him, waiting for the promised assistance of the Normans. But when the Normans came, and Henry retreated, the pope was like the man who prayed for rain and was answered with a flood. The victors, the pope's allies, sacked the city; and, when the citizens resisted, tried to burn it to the ground.

In bitter grief, and amidst the indigna-

tion of the Romans, the liberated pope
retired from the sight of his ruined city
to Salerno. And there, in the midst of a
mighty tempest, the thunder rolling and
the winds howling about him, he died.
The great mastery, whereby the pope had
hoped to rule the world, punishing the
sins of princes, was lost almost before it
was won. "I have loved righteousness,"
he said, "and hated iniquity; therefore I
die in exile."

ANSELM

From an old print

ANSELM

1033-1109

A GREAT fire broke out in the town, as the funeral procession of William the Conqueror entered the gates. Everybody, except the attending clergy, ran to the fire.

When, at last, order was restored, and the service was begun, and the bishop who preached ended his sermon with a prayer for the soul of William, and a hope that if any present had been offended by him they would now forgive him, a man arose and forbade his burial. " The ground on which you stand," he said, " was the place of my father's house, which this man, for whom you make request, took away from my father by violence, and, utterly refusing justice, he, by his strong hand, founded this church. This land, therefore, I claim, and openly demand it back;

and in the behalf of God I forbid the body of the spoiler to be covered with sod that is mine, and to be buried in my inheritance." So they stopped the service, examined the claim and found it just, and paid the man his due.

Even then, at the moment of entombment, the body was found to be too big for the coffin, and was burst asunder as they forced it in.

William the Norman, who avenged upon the English their conquest of the Britons, had ruled England as Charlemagne ruled Europe. He had been supreme. Of Church and State alike, he had been the head. At his will, he had made and unmade nobles; and at his will, he had appointed and dismissed bishops. The great pope Hildebrand, who humbled the emperor at Canossa, and who blessed the banner under which William went to the conquest of England, sent a messenger to the conqueror to re-

ceive his promise of obedience, and
to collect money which was due to
the Church in Rome. William confessed that the money had been carelessly
collected, and said he would do better.
But as to the obedience, he refused to give
it. "Fealty," he said, meaning the service due to a superior, "fealty I neither
have been willing to do, nor will I do it
now, for I never promised it; and I find
not that my predecessors did it to yours."

It was a clear statement of one side of
that tremendous contention between the
Church and the court in which Charlemagne and Hildebrand played their great
parts. There was a man, however, at
William's dreadful funeral who was to
give an equally clear statement of the
other side of the contention, asserting, like
Hildebrand, the supremacy of the Church.
This man was Anselm.

Anselm was a native of Italy. He had
wandered up into the north of France, and

in a day when most men of an earnest or adventurous spirit were either monks or soldiers, he had become a monk. The monastery of Bec had been to him a place, not only of religion, but of education. The prior, Lanfranc, was the greatest schoolmaster of his time. Anselm was his greatest pupil. In the wholesome quiet of the place, beside the stream which ran through the wild woods, Anselm began to think.

Thinking was at that time a disused art. Of course, there was a plenty of the kind of thought which goes along with the planning of campaigns and with the administration of affairs. No man can rule as Charlemagne and William did without being a master of the art of making decisions. But of the persistent study which pursues truth for the joy of pursuing it, and is intent on discovering the meaning of things, there had been little since Augustine. The main work of scholars, in that difficult time when the old empire was going to pieces and the new empire was being built upon its ruins, was to keep the ancient learning safe. Men were busy copying the classic and Christian books of the old time, and teaching them to a new generation. The new generation, in its turn, having been brought out of ignorance by wise men whose knowledge in those times seemed almost supernatural, had grown up in the habit of intellectual submission. The thing to do was to take what the ancients had said, and accept it respectfully. It was true because they said it.

Anselm was profoundly respectful to the ancients, but his mind was not satisfied. He was not content to believe in God because Augustine had believed, or even because St. Paul and St. John had believed. In the quiet of the peaceful abbey, he set himself to establish the truth of the existence of God on the basis of human reason. He took his arguments from the world outside, and from the world within. In the universal idea of God he found a reason for belief in God. The matter is of importance because it was the beginning of philosophy and science in the new era.

Then William took Lanfranc to be archbishop of Canterbury, and his counselor and right hand in his new domains. Anselm became at first prior, and then abbot of Bec. He was as original in the spirit of his discipline as in the manner of his thought. Almost all of the schools of the time were in the monasteries, and in almost every monastery the boys were taught with the book before them and the birch behind them. They were beaten, as a matter of course. At the universities, when young men came up for the degree of bachelor of arts, they were examined, not only as to the progress of their studies, but as to their ability to ply the rod.

Nobody was qualified to teach who did not know how to punish. But to an abbot who complained of the dullness of his pupils Anselm replied that they were made dull by the method of their education. "Day and night," said the discouraged abbot, "we do not cease beating them, and they only get worse." "It is a way to turn men into beasts," said Anselm. "It is like taking a tree and tying back all its branches, and then expecting fruit. Be patient, be kind, be sympathetic."

It was remembered how gentle Anselm was; how he ministered to the sick, to whom food from his hand had a better taste; and how once, in England, a hunted hare sought refuge under his house, and he had the hounds held from hurting it.

Suddenly, this gentle scholar was taken away from the quiet of his books into the midst of the fierce contentions of public life. He was made archbishop of Canterbury.

That great place had been vacant for four years. Lanfranc had died. William had died. William Rufus, his successor, had refused to make an appointment. William Rufus had discovered a new way to make money. The Church in England had grown rich. Sometimes out of gratitude for the blessings of God, sometimes out of interest in religion and desire to strengthen the hands of good men, sometimes in the belief that treasure given to the Church on earth would be credited as treasure in heaven, the great bishoprics and the great monasteries had been given splendid gifts of lands and buildings. But the conquests of Charlemagne in Europe and of William in England had established the theory that all the lands and buildings of the country belonged to the sovereign. He had acquired them by driving out their rightful owners, and had given them away as he pleased, and he claimed the right to take them back.

When the new possessor misbehaved so that the king was angry, he was put out as suddenly as he had come in. This idea that the country belonged to the king was extended by William Rufus to include the property of the Church. And it occurred to him that when for the moment there was no bishop or no abbot to receive the rents, he was himself the proper person to receive them. This pleasant proposition he applied whenever a rich place fell vacant. For four years, accordingly, he had refused to appoint an archbishop of Canterbury, in order to take for his own uses the income of that see.

But William Rufus fell seriously ill. It looked as if he was at the point to die. And he began to think about his sins. They were many in number, for he had been a cruel king like his father, without his father's virtues. He had done all manner of injustice. His prisons were full of the victims of his personal displeasure. And the stolen archbishopric was still in his possession. Among other preparations for a penitent death, he agreed to give that up. He would appoint an archbishop.

The fame of Anselm was already in England, and he himself was at that moment in the country. It was plain to all good people, and to the king, that he was the man for the place. But Anselm was unwilling, partly from distrust of his own strength, partly from reluctance, to leave his quiet prayers and studies. They forced him to it. They brought him by main strength to the sick room of the king. They took the pastoral staff, the symbol of that investiture against which Hildebrand had contended, and tried to thrust it into his closed hand. There was no escape. Only by his acceptance could the long injustice and subjection of the Church be ended.

Thus he became archbishop. And then the king recovered!

Immediately there arose, between Rufus and Anselm, the inevitable debate of that age, the question of mastery. Shall the Church obey the king? or shall the king obey the Church? It turned upon a curious detail. It was the custom for an archbishop to add to his appointment by the king a confirmation by the Roman pope. For this purpose he must go to Rome and there receive a small stole of white wool, marked with four crosses, called a pallium. But when Anselm was appointed, there were two popes, each claiming to be the true one; and England had not yet officially decided between them. When, therefore, Anselm came to Rufus and asked permission to go to Rome to receive the pope's pallium, Rufus said, "To which pope will you go?" Anselm answered, "To pope Urban." "I have not acknowledged Urban," said the king. "That is my matter. By my customs, by the customs of my father, no man may acknowledge a pope in England without my leave. To challenge my power in this is as much as to deprive me of my crown."

Thus the fight began. It was a clear question of authority. Is the Church independent of the king, or not?

On the side of Anselm was the idea of the Church as the representative of righteousness and law. He felt that to surrender was to expose religion to all the disorder and violence of a rude age, and to invite again such robbery as had already been committed by the king. To his mind, the supremacy of the pope over the affairs of England was like what we mean by the supremacy of the Hague Tribunal. It was an exaltation of justice and security over brute strength.

On the side of Rufus was the idea of the independence of the State. Hard and

rough as he was, it was plain to him that
the land must have one sovereign. He
could not share either his responsibility or
his power with any man, however excellent, living in Rome. He could not submit his judgments to any foreign revision.
He must be king in his own land.

Anselm was patient and gentle, but
very determined. A council debated the
matter, but during the excited debates he
was often seen resting his head against a
pillar placidly asleep, and when he waked
he was still of the same mind. The king
contrived to get the pallium sent from
Rome by Urban, but Anselm would not
take it from the king's hands. It was
laid on the altar at Westminster, whence
Anselm took it himself. But, after all,
he insisted on going to Rome, and went.
Rufus at once took possession again of
the revenues of Canterbury, and the wise
pope, while he received Anselm with great
honor, declined to involve himself in the

dispute. The archbishop retired to a little hill-town in Italy, and, with great joy, resumed the simple life of study and prayer which his great office had interrupted. He wrote a book in which he discussed the problems of theology with even greater boldness and originality than before.

Then the news came one day that William Rufus had been killed with an arrow in the New Forest, and Anselm returned to his duties. He returned to contend with Henry as he had contended with Rufus, to go again with his appeal to Rome and to be met, as before, with much respect and little aid, but eventually to conquer Henry. The archbishop threatened to excommunicate the king, as the pope in Hildebrand's time had excommunicated the emperor, and the king yielded. The times were difficult: Robert was making threats from Normandy; the allegiance of many great nobles was very doubtful; the king did not venture to continue the dispute. He yielded. He agreed to surrender the right of the royal investitures of bishops with the ring and staff. They were no longer " his men," as the phrase ran. They were responsible to their own master, the pope in Rome. The date of this victory of Anselm—1107 —is worth remembering. It was the definite beginning of that papal supremacy in England which continued until it was as definitely abolished, in 1534, by Henry VIII.

BERNARD

1091-1153

THE great abbey of Cluny was rich
enough to entertain a king. All the nobles,
all the knights and squires, all the men-
at-arms of a royal retinue could sleep
beneath its hospitable roof, feast in its
noble halls, and pray in its lofty chapel.
Next to Monte Cassino, which Benedict
had founded, it was the most magnificent
religious house in Europe.

There were men, however, to whom
this splendor of the abbey was its shame.
They compared the architecture of Monte
Cassino with that cave in the cliff where
Benedict had begun to live his holy life.
They remembered that Cluny had been
established by devout monks who disliked
the luxury of the Benedictines, and wished
to return to the simplicity and severity of

VIRGIN AND ST. BERNARD

From the painting by Filippino Lippi, Badia, Florence

the ancient rule. They determined to repeat that good endeavor, and do it better. One of them retreated, accordingly, to a solitary place in a forest whose Latin name was Cistercium, and there entered into the hardships which his soul desired. He lived like a soldier between battles. He kept watch as one who expects an enemy. He maintained a daily drill of the spirit. He contended against the devil.

But for a long time only a few went with him. When he died, his little monastery was the humblest and poorest in France. His successor grew discouraged. It seemed as if the good days of the strict life were passed, and as if there were no longer any who cared to keep the rule which, to the saints, had been a way to heaven, steep but sure. At last, one day, there came in through the forest a company of twenty-five or thirty men. They stopped at the door of Cistercium, and asked to be admitted. They desired to be Cistercians.

The leader of this group was a tall youth, with yellow hair and reddish beard, whose name was Bernard. In the company were his four brothers, and the rest of the number were his relatives and friends. He had persuaded them to leave the world, and to undertake the monastic life in earnest. He had inspired them with his own ideals. To these recruits, Bernard added others. He had the persuasive eloquence of one who has found the supreme joy of life and wishes to impart it to his neighbors. Nobody ever lived who took more real delight in going without food and sleep that he might say his prayers and strengthen his soul; and such was the enthusiasm with which he described the charm of the monastic life that mothers hid their sons when Bernard came into their neighborhood, to keep them from hearing his convincing words.

He appealed to the best hopes of high-
minded young men, who were looking for
a life of romance and adventure. They
would find it, he said, in the abbey of
Cistercium.

Pretty soon the little monastery was so
crowded that they began to send out
colonies. One colony, of which Bernard
was the leader, went through the forests a
hundred miles to a wild valley which a
knight had given to the monks out of his
estate. The valley was filled with thick
woods, through which ran a little river.
The hills came near together at the west,
and there they settled, building a rude
house. Before them to the east lay the
widening valley, eight miles long. Year
by year, cutting down trees, draining
marshes, clearing land for gardens and
pastures, planting vines on the hills on
one side and orchards on the hills on the
other side, digging a pond for fish, building, not only a chapel, but a mill, they

civilized the place, and made Clairvaux,—
for that was the name of it,—one of the
fairest habitations in the world. Nobody
left it without longing to return.

This was not done, however, without
great labor and privation. There was a
" starving time " at Clairvaux, as there was
afterwards at Jamestown and Plymouth.
It is a part of the adventures of colonists.
Depending wholly on themselves, and beginning too late in the season to get food
out of the earth, they lived during the
first winter on beechnuts. But they liked
it. Bernard delighted in it. Even when
better times came, and they had good crops
and good fruits, he kept to a fare so simple that he was in danger of starvation.
He lost all sense of taste, and perceived
no difference between wine and oil. Happily, a good doctor took him in charge,
and saved his life, though he was too
late to save his health.

Bernard was absolutely unselfish. He

had no plans for personal advantage. He desired nothing, neither money, nor comfort, nor power, nor reputation. Nobody could rob him. Nobody could influence his thought or act by any threat or promise. In those days when every knight was fighting to increase his possessions, and almost every abbot,—as at Monte Cassino and Cluny,—was trying to widen his lands and erect new buildings and was in search of more money for these purposes, the appearance of Bernard was an extraordinary fact. He was the most independent man of his time; and he became the most influential. Selfish as men were, they were still able to appreciate unselfishness. They saw the value of the opinion and judgment of a man whose mind was not affected by any consideration other than the will of God, as he understood it.

The result was that during the lifetime of Bernard the spiritual capital of Europe was at Clairvaux. Of course, the monastery grew tremendously. Bernard saw sixty-five colonies go out to found new abbeys. But the glory and the might of it all was the personality of this humble, modest, and self-sacrificing man. That which Hildebrand at Rome, and Anselm at Canterbury, had claimed by right of office, came to Bernard without office and without claim, because of the righteousness of his life and the purity of his soul. He was called to kings' courts, and was given the final decision of questions on which the peace of Europe depended. But he declined all offers of high position, and went back from these great errands to take his place again at Clairvaux, working in the fields like Columba, feeding the pigs, greasing his own boots.

One time, a French duke, grandfather of Richard-of-the-Lion-Heart, rich as a great king, vicious in life and uncontrolled in temper, took his part in the continual fight between the Church and the world, by removing certain good bishops and putting bad ones in their places. To the demand of the pope that he should restore the faithful bishops, he returned a stout defiance. Nobody could do anything with him. Everybody was afraid of him. Bernard came from Clairvaux, weak in body, unattended by any physical force, and met the duke at a church door, and scared him into a fit. The man fell upon the ground and foamed at the mouth. "Here," said Bernard, "is one of the bishops whom you have deposed. Take him back to his place; and do the same with all the others." And the duke obeyed.

Another time, Bernard met upon the road a group of men in the midst of whom was one with a halter about his neck, being led to be hanged for robbery and murder. The abbot asked for the man, led him gently to Clairvaux, dressed him in the garments of a monk, placed him in the quiet company of the brethren, and saved him, body and soul.

It happened, in Bernard's time, that the whole Church was again divided by the contention of two men, each of whom claimed to be the truly elected pope. The election had been a scene of disorder. Hildebrand had put an end to the old method whereby the pope had been elected at a Roman town-meeting, and had confined the voting to certain rectors of Roman parishes, and bishops of neighboring dioceses, called cardinals. But on this occasion some of the cardinals had elected Anacletus, and others had elected Innocent. Each claimed that the other meeting was illegal. The fine theory of Anselm that the pope is the representative of law and order was imperiled by this situation. The two claimants were fighting vigorously; Anacletus had driven Innocent out of Italy; the voice of law and order must be sought elsewhere.

The king of France called an assembly of bishops and abbots to consider this great matter. And the king and the assembly summoned Bernard. He was made arbiter of the rival claims. The whole nation, and other nations, awaited his decision. He examined the conditions of the election but, still more carefully, the character of the men. He set aside the legal details, and chose for pope the claimant who seemed to him the better man. He selected Innocent. That choice determined France, and further appeals of Bernard determined Germany and England. Innocent became pope.

The new pope visited Clairvaux and was there welcomed, so the old chronicle says, "not by banquets but by virtues." He found a church with bare walls, no pictures, no stained glass; an altar with iron candlesticks and a silver chalice; priests in linen vestments, singing the service with the utmost simplicity; and the rule so carefully kept in the refectory that beans and pease were the chief food on the table, there was no wine, and the only fish which appeared was served as a special dainty to the pope. Afterwards, when another pope, one of the old pupils of Bernard, came to visit him, they gave him the only fowl which they had in the pantry. These glimpses show at its best that Cistercian revival of the monastic life which links the name of Bernard with that of Benedict. What it came to, in its turn, appears in "Ivanhoe" in the person of the Cistercian prior Aymer.

After the settlement of the contention of the rival popes, the next event which stirred the heart of Christendom was the second Crusade.

Peter the Hermit had preached the first Crusade at the Council of Clermont, when Bernard was but four years old. He must have remembered from his childhood the vast movement of that army in which all the strength of Europe seemed to be enlisted; and the stories of his youth must have been tales which were told by knights and palmers after that ill-fated expedition.

The first Crusade had succeeded in taking Jerusalem out of the hands of the Turks. It had established Christian garrisons in Antioch and Edessa. In the midst of horrible suffering, avenged by cruelty as horrible, and in spite of all manner of contradiction of the most important principles of Christian living, the Crusade had assisted to civilize Europe. It had called the various nations together for a common purpose; it had widened their experience of the world; and it had brought back into the still savage social life of the West some of the refinement of the East.

But now news came of the capture of Edessa. That Christian stronghold had fallen before the might of the Turks, and its loss was a prophecy of the taking of Jerusalem. The Holy City, won by the shedding of the best blood of Europe, was in peril. It was time for a second crusade. So thought Louis VIII. of France, who had just come back sick at heart and stricken in conscience from a little war in which he had burned alive a thousand people in a church. So thought the Knights Templars vowed to the defense of the Holy Sepulcher, and eager for martial exercise. So thought the pope, and Bernard.

Bernard was to the second Crusade what Peter the Hermit had been to the first. He was its preacher. Mounted on a wooden pulpit, facing a vast multitude under the open sky, slight in figure, but strong in voice, and terrible in his mighty earnestness, he called for volunteers to fight, as he said, for Christ. And again, as at the beginning, there was a tearing of red cloaks for badges, Bernard setting

the example. Again, all over Europe,
men were taking the Cross. Women were
sending spinning-wheels to knights who
were too timid or too sensible to go, suggesting that these were more to their taste
than the swords of heroes. Armies were
being mustered, drilled, and set to march-
ing. Again the land was bereft of its
best strength. Out of every family, a hus-
band, father, brother, son, was on his way
to Palestine. And Bernard, in city after
city, was threatening the pains of hell to
such as stayed at home, and promising the
bliss of heaven to such as took the Cross
and went.

But the second Crusade failed like the
first, and worse. The Greek emperor at
Constantinople resented the Latin invasion.
He hated the Crusade. He gave the
armies guides who led them into hopeless
deserts where they died of thirst. The
Turks attacked them. Finally, they took
to flight and such as were fortunate made

their broken way back to their homes. And the grief and indignation of the widows and children of Europe fell upon the head of the man whose sermons had sent these armies to defeat and death.

Even here, Bernard was still master. With all his self-reproach, he had the consciousness of having followed what honestly seemed to him the will of God. And this honesty was recognized. People saw that he had made the great mistake for no gain of his own. He returned to his cloister, and took up again his quiet life of prayer and study. He wrote letters to great people; he answered the questions of the perplexed; he indicated what he thought to be the righteous direction of public affairs. Great and little, he interested himself in all matters in which a decision must be made for the right or the wrong. One of his last letters was addressed to a count whose vassals had

stolen some of the pigs of Clairvaux. " If
they had been my own," he said, " it had
not greatly mattered; I was taking care
of them for a neighbor. You must replace
them."

BECKET

1118-1170

THE story of St. Martin and his cloak was repeated one day—with a difference—in the streets of London.

The king and the chancellor were riding together in the cold winter, when they saw, in the way ahead of them, a poor man coming down the road, hugging his tattered coat about him, shivering in the bitter wind. "Do you see that poor man?" says the king. "Yes, I see him," says the chancellor, "he is very cold." "He shivers," says the king, "his clothes are thin and ragged. Would it not be a kind and Christian act to give him a warm cloak?" "Indeed, it would," says the chancellor, "and it is mighty good of your Majesty to think of it." So they came up with the man, and stopped their horses,

BECKET.

From an old print

and the king said: " Friend, you seem very cold; would you not like a thick warm cloak about your shoulders? " And the man, who knew them not, and doubted whether the words were meant in jest or earnest, answered that a thick warm cloak would be a comfortable thing to have. "Then take this one," says the king, laughing, and he began to pull the chancellor's cloak from off his back,—a fine cloak of warm cloth, gray and scarlet. The chancellor held on tight to the cloak, and the king pulled hard, and the knights and nobles of the company came clattering up on their horses to see what all the bustle was about. At last, the chancellor gave way, and the astonished poor man had the cloak.

The king was Henry II., the chancellor was Thomas Becket. This was only one of many times when they played together like boys. The king used to go over to Becket's house to see what he had for dinner, and if it looked better than what he was likely to get at home,—and it did often, for the chancellor lived in splendid state,—the king would vault over the table, and seat himself in the best place, without waiting for an invitation. Sometimes he went for business, sometimes for fun. The two were always together. "Never in Christian times," says an old chronicle, "were there two men more of one mind, or better friends." The king was young, and the chancellor was younger still.

Becket was the son of a merchant who had come from France and had established a profitable business in London. His father had given him a good education, and he had made the most of it. The lad was quick to learn, and what he learned he remembered. He studied law and theology, and was trained also in the exercises of knighthood. He could take his part with grace and strength in

the great game of the tournament, with
lance and sword. He was tall and slim,
with a pale face and black hair, and was
most pleasant to look upon. Everybody
liked him. To the knowledge of a
scholar, he added the manners of a
courtier. He had a frank and winning
way, and the things which he said, with a
bit of a stammer, were good to hear.
Wherever he went, he made friends.

Then his father failed in his business,
and Thomas came home and went into a
lawyer's office, for a time, as clerk. But
he was brought to the attention of the
archbishop of Canterbury, who took him
into his employ. And thus he proceeded
from one position to another, entirely on
his merits and good looks, serving always
diligently and well, till he became archdeacon. Those were days when the clergy
had a great many other things to do beside saying prayers and preaching sermons. They were lawyers as well as min-

isters.   An archdeacon was a kind of judge.   Thus, by an easy and natural promotion, the archdeacon, having• come to the knowledge of the king, was by him appointed chancellor.

Thus Becket became both rich and powerful.   He came into possession of great estates.   He had charge of the king's seal, and all the royal documents and decrees were signed by him.   He was the third person in the realm of England; first, the king; second, the archbishop; third, the chancellor.

One time, he went on a pleasant em· bassy to France.   Henry desired to ask the hand of the French king's daughter in marriage for his son.   He sent Becket to represent him.   The splendor of the ambassador's retinue amazed the country. First, as they marched, came singing boys, two hundred and fifty of them, ten abreast; then the chancellor's hunting dogs, greyhounds in leash, and hunts-

men with them; then eight carriages, each
drawn by five horses, bearing the furniture of the chancellor's chapel, and of
his chamber, and of his kitchen; then
sumpter-horses carrying his chests of
gold and silver plate, his store of money,
the sacred vessels of his private altar, and
his four-and-twenty changes of raiment.
Under each sumpter-wagon walked a
chained dog, big and terrible as a lion,
and on the back of each horse rode a
tailed monkey. Then came the squires
with shields, and knights in shining armor
riding two and two, and, last of all, the
magnificent chancellor. All the roads
were lined with people; all the windows,
as they passed, were filled with spectators.
And all who beheld the glittering procession said,—as the chancellor intended
them to say,—" Marvelous is the king of
the English, whose chancellor goeth thus
and so grandly!"

Becket went again to France on an

errand not so pleasant. There was a war between the English and the French, and he carried over seven hundred knights, with five thousand soldiers behind them, and he at the head, and fought a forty days' campaign, winning great victories. Once, "with horse at charge and lance in rest," he met in single combat a French knight of renown, whom he overthrew. And ever in battle he was among those who dared the most.

One story, in the midst of this courtly splendor and knightly valor, shows that Becket had a mind for other things. A man who had affairs which he wished to bring to the attention of the king sought to lay his matters first,—as the custom was,—before the chancellor. But, getting to London too late in the day for such business, he postponed his errand until morning. He rose early, and, passing a church on his way, he went in to say his prayers. The place was empty, except for one other devout person, who was kneeling by the door. The stranger's attention was attracted by the earnestness of this worshiper's prayer, and he observed him carefully. As he chanced, however, to cough or sneeze, the man who was at his prayers, thus perceiving that he was not alone, brought his petitions to an end, and left the church. When presently, the stranger carried his business to the chancellor's court, there, on the chancellor's bench, sat the person whom he had seen at his devotions.

Now, it was the desire of Henry to bring the nation under his own control. It was a wild, rough time, when many men did as they pleased without regard to peace or justice, and there was need of a firm hand. The king, very properly, felt that it was his business to govern England, and he proposed to do it.

But in those days there were two kinds of law: one law for people in general, and another law for the clergy. There were two kinds of courts: the king's court and the Church's court. And the clergy, who were subject only to the Church's court, included most of the people who could read and write. All the lawyers were clergymen, all the schoolmasters, and most of the men in public office.

The consequence was that the king was the ruler of only a part of the nation. The real ruler of the other part was the pope in Rome. And this made great confusion, and was constantly in the way of the king's purpose to bring the whole land under one strong law. A man might be a most dangerous citizen, and guilty of most serious offenses, but if he belonged in any way to the estate of the clergy, if he was a monk or even a sexton, the king could not touch him.

So when the archbishop of Canterbury died, the king saw an opportunity to end this confusion, and to bring the

Church under the law of the State. He appointed Becket in his place. "Now," he said to himself, "Becket and I will work together." The splendid chancellor, the king's friend, loving power and wealth and luxury, would be the very man to compel the Church to obey the king's will.

But there was a quality in Becket which the king had never noticed. He had a strong sense of loyalty to whatever master he served. He had been devoted to the king, and at his bidding had already disregarded what seemed to be the interest of the Church. He had compelled churchmen to pay taxes which they had not been used to pay. He had served the king completely. But that was because he was the servant of the king. Now, as archbishop, he considered himself the servant of the pope. The man was made that way. That was how his conscience worked.

He begged the king not to appoint him. He looked down at his splendid dress, and said, " I am not the man to be set in this holy office. I know, too, that if I take it, the pleasant friendship between us shall surely end in bitterness. You will demand what I cannot grant." But the king insisted.

Then Becket changed his life. He put off his gay apparel. He fasted and prayed. He gave himself to the Church, as he had previously given himself to the court.

The king called a council which passed laws bringing all men, whether clergy or not, under the control of the king's judges. He restored the old custom of investiture against which Anselm had contended. He required every bishop to confess himself the " king's man." And, especially, he decreed that whenever anybody was convicted in the Church court, he must be sent at once to the king's court for punishment. Against the enactments of this council Becket protested. He was honestly convinced that the welfare of the nation rested on the independence of the Church.

Thus it was Becket against Henry, Church against State. All the king's fine plans for good government were stopped. The strife divided England for the moment into two nations: on one side, Henry and the barons; on the other side, Becket and the pope. Each was trying to control the other; each was contending for independence. So it went on for six years. Henry attacked the Church by taking away its lands; Becket attacked the State by excommunicating those who were against him. At that time, people believed that excommunication placed men in peril of everlasting punishment. They were afraid of it. Becket, who had fled to France, refused all compromise. He would not agree to any proposition of the king except with the reservation, "saving the honor of my order." That meant that he would not yield in the slightest degree the independence of the Church. Even those who were on Becket's side grew weary of the sound of the words. "Come up," cried one, as his horse stumbled,—"saving the honor of my order."

At last, the king and the archbishop met in France, and a sort of peace was made between them, and Becket returned to Canterbury. Immediately, he began the fight again. The king's young son had been crowned, during Becket's absence, by the archbishop of York. But a royal coronation, according to the custom, was the business of the archbishop of Canterbury. Becket excommunicated the bishops who had been concerned in it. Thus nothing had been gained. The king was as far from his great plans as ever.

The news of these doings came to the

king in France. And one of those who stood about him said, "My lord, while Thomas lives, you will not have peace or quiet, or see another good day." And the king answered in fierce anger, "I have nourished and promoted sluggish and wretched knaves," he said, "who are faithless to their lord, and suffer him to be tricked thus infamously by a low clerk."

Thereupon four knights of the king's household departed straightway from his presence, saying no word to any man, and made their way to England. On the fourth day after Christmas they came to Canterbury and confronted the archbishop. "You have presumed," they said, "to excommunicate the bishop by whom the king's son was crowned. You have made yourself a traitor to the prince and to the king. Now take back these curses, or else depart out of the land." And when he refused either to change his curses into blessings, or to depart, they threatened his life. They would go and arm themselves, they said, and come back and kill him. "Here," he answered, "here shall ye find me."

And there, indeed, they found him. The bell rang for vespers. In the choir of the great church the monks began to sing the service. The archbishop joined them in their prayers. There came a great battering of swords and lances at the door, and the four knights entered. In the late afternoon, and at the season when the days are short, the church was dark, except where candles glimmered in the choir. "Where is Thomas Becket?" cried the knights. "Where is the traitor to the king and realm?" And when the service suddenly ceased, and the frightened monks begged Becket to take advantage of the dark and hide himself, they cried again, "Where is the archbishop?" Then came Becket forth. "You shall die,' they shouted. "I am ready to die," he answered, "for my Lord, that in my blood the Church may obtain liberty and peace." Then they struck him with their swords, and escaped into the night.

The murder of Becket horrified all Christendom, but nobody was more filled with horror than the king. He put off his royal robes, and put on sackcloth. Such was his grief that those about him feared that he would lose his reason, or his life. He submitted himself to the judgment of the pope. He agreed to send a hundred knights to fight in the Holy Land against the Saracens, to restore the lands which he had taken from the Church, and to repeal the laws against which Becket had contended. And one day, at Canterbury, he laid himself down on the church floor and directed the monks to beat him, each with a rod.

As for the martyr, extraordinary things began to happen at his tomb. Sick people were made sound, and the lame began to walk, and the blind to see. The pope placed the name of Becket among the saints. A golden shrine was erected over him, which year by year grew in magnificence. The glory of the magnificent chancellor was eclipsed by the splendor of the saint. Gold and precious gems surrounded him. Pilgrims came from far and near to say their prayers beside him, hoping that he would add his prayers to theirs. Chaucer's pleasant company, telling the Canterbury Tales, was but one of the thousand groups of men and women who came to see the place of the martyrdom of Becket.

LANGTON

From the statue by Gutzon Borglum, Cathedral of
St John the Divine, New York

LANGTON

THE great fight of Becket against King Henry for the independence of the Church was followed by the great fight of Langton against King John for the independence of the nation.

John had been false to his father Henry. The last days of that strong king had been embittered by the rebellion of his older sons. John, the youngest, was his favorite. For John's sake, Henry had disowned Richard and had made war against him. But when the battles went against the king, and the victorious nobles brought him a list of the rebels whom he must pardon, the name at the head of the list was that of John. Then the sick king turned his face to the wall. "Now," he said, "let things go as they will,—I care no more for myself or for the world."

John had been false also to his brother Richard. You remember the message from the king of France which came to John as he sat at the tournament of Ashby-de-la-Zouche: "The devil is loose; take care of yourself." Richard-of-the-Lion-Heart had been fighting in Palestine, trying to take Jerusalem out of the hands of Saladin. Shipwrecked on his way home, he had been seized by his enemies, and held for ransom in Germany. Meanwhile, in England, John had been trying to become king of England in his place. The "devil" was Richard, released from prison, returning to his throne.

Then Richard died, killed with an arrow at the siege of a town in France, and John, becoming king indeed, began to show himself as false to his people as he had been false to his father and his brother. The man who stood against him, and saved the country, was Stephen Langton.

The kings of England since the Norman Conquest had been Frenchmen. Their kingdom had included, not England only, but rich lands in France. And in France they had lived, coming but rarely to England, partly for the purpose of fighting against rebellious English, and partly for the purpose of getting English money with which to fight rebellious Frenchmen. But when John became king, most of the French possessions had been lost. Therefore he lived, much against his will, in England.

John's great desire was to get back the provinces of France. But for such a war he needed men and money. He found his demand for money met by the refusal of the bishops, and his demand for men met by the refusal of the barons. The bishops declared that they would not pay the king's taxes; the barons declared that they would no longer fight the king's battles over seas.

The king's struggle with the Church began with the appointment of an archbishop of Canterbury. That great place being vacant, there were two men proposed to fill it. One was chosen by the monks of Canterbury at their own will; another was chosen by the monks of Canterbury acting against their own will at the command of the king. One was the Church's man, the other was the king's man. The two appealed to the pope. But the pope, at that moment, was Innocent III., whose supreme ideal was to carry into effect the principles of Hildebrand. He proposed to be the spiritual father of all Europe, having all kings for his sons, and securing thereby the peace and righteousness of Christendom. Innocent, accordingly, dismissed both of the applicants for the archbishopric of Canterbury, and appointed Stephen Langton.

Langton was an Englishman, of high character, then resident in Rome, who for his merits had been made a cardinal.

The king refused to permit Langton to enter England, and the pope threatened an interdict. Now, in the Middle Ages, an interdict was considered worse than a war and a plague combined. It was a withdrawal of the privileges of the Christian religion from all the people of the land; once an interdict was pronounced at Rome, all church bells ceased to ring, all church doors were closed. There were no more services, and no more sacraments. Nobody could be baptized, nobody could receive the saving grace of the Holy Communion, nobody could be married, nobody could be buried. It meant to the people, not only an interruption of all the rites of religion on which they depended, but the serious peril of their immortal souls.

Innocent threatened to lay England

under an interdict till John should receive
Langton. And when the archbishop of
York was in his turn driven out of the
country for his resistance to an unjust tax,
the threat was executed. First the land
was laid under the interdict; then the king
was excommunicated; finally, the king was
declared deposed, his throne was pronounced vacant, all his subjects were
absolved from their obedience to him, all
his enemies were encouraged to attack him,
and in particular his worst enemy, Philip
of France, was commanded to make war
upon him.

Then John found himself in evil case.
At first, he was defiant enough, and tried
the fortunes of war, but his barons would
not fight, and the war went against him.
Then he submitted. He knelt before
Pandulph, the representative of the pope.
He took off his royal crown and put it
into Pandulph's hands. He confessed himself the " pope's man." And to the pope

he gave all England, as a conquered king surrenders his kingdom to his conqueror. The interdict was removed and Stephen Langton came to Canterbury.

Immediately Langton became the head not of the bishops only but of the barons.

The first thing which he did, when he released the king from his excommunication, was to make him swear to keep the laws of Edward the Confessor. That meant that the king must observe the ancient customs by which the liberties of Englishmen were protected before the Normans conquered England. It speedily became plain, however, that this was too vague a promise. Having such a king as John, it was necessary to make the rights of the people much more definite. John had inherited, from his Norman ancestors, the idea that the kingdom belonged to the king. They had taken England by force, and they proposed to do what they pleased with it. The king's will, they said, was law. But the new England, which had grown up since the Conquest, was now unwilling to consent to this. The despotism of the foreign kings had united all the races of the lands. It had made Angles and Saxons, Britons and Danes, Englishmen and Normans, into one people. And this people, with Langton for its spokesman and leader, was at last arrayed against the king.

Thus the great interdict was followed by the Great Charter.

Suddenly, to the surprise of John, the barons met in arms and demanded a new statement of the relation between the king and the people. They proposed a series of laws which should thenceforth govern, not only the people, but the king. These laws, based on old customs and traditions much improved by experience, were drawn up by Langton for the king to sign.

The king postponed and postponed this surrender of his despotic power. He ap-

pealed for help to his new master, the
pope, under whose protection he had
hoped to overcome his enemies. But the
pope sent him no help. The bishops were
against him, the barons were against him,
the people were against him. He was
alone against this demand for the liberties
of the land. Thus he submitted to England as he had before submitted to Rome.

The place of meeting was an island in
the Thames near Windsor. The king and
his courtiers were encamped on one bank
of the river, Langton and the barons were
encamped on the other side, in a wide
meadow, whose name of Runnymede has
been famous since that day in the history
of political liberty. There John signed
the Great Charter, "Magna Charter."
And after he had signed it, back he went
to his palace, and there rolled upon the
floor in a rage for which he had no words,
gnawing the sticks and straws.

The charter provided for the freedom of

the Church from the personal will of the king. It secured all men from imprisonment or seizure except by process of law. It declared that no new tax should be imposed except by consent of the common council of the realm. And a committee of twenty-four stout and determined barons was appointed to see that the king obeyed it.

It is true that the pope declared the charter was of no effect. But that was not because of any affection for John or because of any objection to the liberties of England. It was because he felt that he should have been consulted first. That was according to his honest theory of the proper conduct of the world. It is true that Langton was recalled to Rome. But it made no difference. The great thing was done.

ST. DOMINIC

From the picture by Titian, Villa Borghese, Rome

DOMINIC

1170-1221

ONE of the most dangerous things in the world is money; and equally dangerous is power.

Both power and money are very pleasant possessions, but they tempt people to be selfish. Men who become rich often forget that they have neighbors who are poor; and they who have power are disposed to use it for their own advantage. They live in their comfortable houses, and attend to their own business, and shut their eyes and ears to the hardships of the world. They are tempted to be worse than selfish. Being attired in purple and fine linen, and faring sumptuously every day, they forget not their neighbors only, but God also. And this has happened, not only to princes, but to priests; not only to barons, but to bishops, and has made its way into monasteries.

It was very fine for Hildebrand to take the crown of the emperor of Germany, and for Innocent to take the crown of the king of England. It was the honest belief of these popes that if they could thus make themselves the masters of the world they could make it a good world. But such mastery brought with it the perils of power and money, and the great, rich Church fell into selfishness and evil living. The cathedrals and the abbeys were splendid buildings, and the services which took place in them were magnificent with colors and lights and incense, but the ministers who conducted the services and the people who attended them made little effort to make either the world or themselves better. " The time has long passed," said one cardinal to another, " when the Church could say, with Peter, ' Silver and gold have I none.' " " Yes," replied the other cardinal, " and the time has also passed when the Church could say, ' Rise up and walk.' "

This state of things produced a reaction. There were still great numbers of good people who saw clearly that the true purpose of religion is to help men and women to live aright with God and with their neighbors. The sight of the Church of Christ forsaking its proper work in the world, devoting itself to architecture and music, and living in selfishness and sin, filled them with horror. They hated it. By-and-by the time came when the Church had so far departed from the Christian religion that they felt themselves forced into that great revolution called the Reformation, but, long before that, they cried out, in the name of God, like the old prophets, against a religion which had come to be, in many places, only a combination of idolatry and immorality.

Thus in the south of France, in the neighborhood of the city of Albi, arose the Albigenses.

It is difficult to determine just what these people believed. Almost all that is known about them is contained in the accounts of their enemies. Very likely, they had strange opinions. They were reported to hold, like the Manichees of St. Augustine's day, that there is a bad God as well as a good God. That was their explanation of the wickedness of the world as they saw it. It is certain that they were enemies of the Church, and that their enmity was based on moral grounds. They were good, earnest people who loved righteousness and hated iniquity. They stopped going to church, and held meetings of their own. They went about preaching what seemed to them the true religion. The churches were deserted. The people who desired to live aright joined the Albigenses. The Church sent missionaries, men of that Cistercian Order to which St. Bernard had belonged,—but the missionaries were dignified persons, dressed in splendid clothes, and taking excellent care of themselves, and they were in such contrast with the plain, simple, and devout Albigensian preachers that they made no converts.

At that time, however, a young man was journeying through that part of the country, with open eyes and an understanding heart. Dominic had just been graduated at a Spanish university, and was taking his first look at the world. He was an excellent scholar, of pure and helpful life, and desirous to be of use in the Church. He saw at once that the elegant Cistercians could accomplish nothing. What was needed was a company of men, living as plainly and righteously as the Albigensians, who could preach with all the Albigensian directness and with more wisdom. He saw that the revolt of the

people against the Church was caused by
the wickedness and weakness of the
Church, and that their departures from
the creed were caused by errors which
clear explanation might correct. The
Church must be represented, then, by
better men, and the truth must be correctly
taught.

The men whom Dominic gathered about
him for this excellent purpose became
presently a new society called the Dominicans. They brought back into religion
the ancient custom of preaching. It had
fallen into disuse. Bishops preached,
but hardly anybody else; and even the
bishops preached little, except in Lent.
The purpose of going to church
was not to hear a sermon, but to attend a service. The Dominicans were
preachers.

Dominic introduced another new idea
into the religion of his time. The Benedictines and the Cistercians lived in

monasteries; their ideal was to keep themselves apart from the world. The Dominicans took a new name. Instead of calling themselves " monks," which means men living alone, they called themselves "friars," which means brothers. They lived out-of-doors. They went about among the people.

Dominic's mother had a queer dream one night, in which she saw her son changed into a little black-and-white dog, having a blazing torch in his mouth. The black-and-white part of the dream seemed to come true when the Dominicans chose for their dress a long white cassock, over which they wore a black cloak. But a blazing torch may serve either to give light or to set fire.

The good purpose of Dominic was to enlighten the world. His intention was to advance the cause of truth by the use of reason. The bad world, he thought, would be made better by the persuasion of earnest preaching. This, however, is a slow process, and calls for long patience. Nobody knows what the eloquence of the Dominicans might have done for the Albigenses, because the sermons of Dominic were speedily followed by the sword of Simon de Montfort. The pope proclaimed a crusade against these critics of the Church. An orthodox army was sent against them. The faithful preachers and their good people were murdered,—men, women, and children together,—in the ruins of their burning houses. The blazing torch burned city after city. At last, the Albigenses ceased to raise their protest against the sins of the Church, because scarcely any of them were left alive. Thus the selfish and evil Church met the first determined effort to restore the righteousness of true religion.

And after the horrors of the Albigensian Crusade, came the horrors of the Inquisition. People who denied the faith, or

who were suspected of denying the faith,
were examined by inquisitors, put to torture, whipped, pinched with hot iron,
their legs and arms broken, their skin
scraped off, their tongues cut out, their
eyes burned in the sockets, and, at last,
tied to 'a stake, the blazing torch set fire
to the heap of wood in the midst of which
the heretic was fastened. It used to be
said that Dominic established the Inquisition. Probably not. It is certain, however, that the bad business of managing it
was in the hands of the Dominicans.
They addressed themselves to the putting
down of heresy. They were the defenders
of the faith. They preached, indeed, following the example of their founder.
They wrote books. One of them, Thomas
Aquinas, was the greatest theologian of
the Middle Ages. Everywhere, their
churches and houses stood beside the
churches and houses of the Franciscans;
the Dominicans devoted to orthodoxy, the

Franciscans to charity. But they conducted the Inquisition.

Thus the ideals of Dominic were brought to failure. He belongs with Francis, with Wycliffe, and with Wesley in his intention to save the world by preaching; but his preachers proved to be only the heralds of the most infamous of the wars of the Church. He belongs with modern men in his purpose to meet error with the weapons of reason; but the movement which began with reason proceeded to deal with error after a fashion in which reason had no part whatever. It was the chief enemy of reason. Dominic was a good man, whose single aim was to serve God and the Church. He succeeded in bringing a new earnestness into religion. But that which in him was earnestness in his followers was bigotry and cruelty. The virtues of Dominic are obscured by the crimes of the Dominicans.

FRANCIS
1182-1226

OF all the merry lads in the sunny streets of Assisi, the merriest was young Francis Bernardone. He it was who sang the liveliest songs, and wore the gayest clothes, and was the leader of the games. His father was a merchant whose shop was filled with silk and cloth of gold, and there was money for Francis to spend, and he spent it splendidly. He worked, too, in the shop, and carried his father's goods into the market of Assisi, and into other markets, even so far away as Rome.

Assisi stands on a hilltop, and one looks out over some of the fairest fields of Italy, away to Perugia on another hilltop, neighbor and rival, with whose citizens the Assisans used to fight whenever opportunity offered. It was thus made plain

to Francis, even from the beginning of
his life, that Assisi was not the whole of
the world. And this important fact his
journeys into other towns confirmed. In
one of the battles with Perugia he was
taken captive, and lay for a whole year
in a Perugian prison. Thus amidst his
merriment, he had time to think.

One day, in Rome, going into St. Peter's
Church, and noticing there the careful
economy with which the worshipers made
their offerings to God, he took his
purse and threw down all he had before
an altar, the gold and silver making a
great clattering upon the floor. Then he
changed clothes with a beggar on the
church steps, and there sat all day and
begged.

Twice, after an illness, he dreamed
strange dreams which seemed to tell him
what he ought to do with his life.

One was the vision of a great armory
full of swords and lances, into which he

was bidden to go and arm himself. He
thought that this meant that he should
be a soldier, and out he started on the
next expedition, with shield and helmet,
mounted on horseback. But he came back,
convinced that soldiering was not the trade
for him.

The other dream commanded him to re-
build a ruined church, and at once he set
about the work of making a new wall for
the little chapel of St. Darnian. He went
around asking his neighbors to give him
stones.

It was this rebuilding of St. Darnian's
which sent Francis finally upon his great
career. The repairing even of a small
ruined church without money, and with
no other labor than that of one pair of
unaccustomed hands, is a slow process.
Francis grew impatient. One day, filled
with a great desire to get on with this
good work, he took a lot of bales of
cloth out of his father's store, and rode

away to the next town, and sold both cloth and horse. "There," he said to the priest of St. Darnian's, "take this money for the church." But the priest was not willing to take it, fearing the displeasure of Francis's father. Francis, too, as he considered the matter, began to see that his father might object to this selling of his goods. He tossed the money into a corner, and hid himself. And, indeed, his father did object most seriously. His neighbors also felt that Francis had done wrong. When, at last, he ventured out of hiding and made his way to his home, they hooted him in the streets, said he was crazy, and stoned him, till, as he drew near the house, his father came out to see what all the noise might mean, and, finding Francis, seized him, dragged him in, and locked him up.

Francis was not a boy when these events took place. He was twenty-five years old. Of course, it was not right for him to take things out of his father's store and sell them, even for the Church, but he naturally felt, after years of service, that the business belonged in part to him. Anyhow, he was not penitent, and one day when his mother, in love and pity, let him out, back he went to St. Darnian's.

And then his father went to law about it. He appealed to the magistrates to get his money back. The matter was referred to the bishop. The bishop wisely advised the young man to restore the money to his father; and this he did, gathering it up from the dusty corner where he had thrown it. But when he brought it to his father, he brought his clothes also. He took off his fine garments, piled them on the floor and put the money on top. "Now," he cried, "I am the servant of God, and my father is the Father who is in heaven."

The bishop flung a cloak about him, and somebody gave him clothes to wear, and his lodging was at St. Darnian's. The good priest gave him food, and, mindful of the gay feasts in which he had delighted, gave him some dainties with it. For Francis, who was always a boy to the end of his life, confessed long after that he had never lost his early liking for sweet things. But when Francis saw the dainties, he perceived that he had not even yet given up the luxuries of life. Immediately, he took a plate and went out and begged his food from door to door.

From that moment, Francis was independently poor. Gradually, companions came to him, first one and then another, wishing to share his life, and he required them all to give up everything that they possessed The idea of a great society had not come into his mind, but it was plain already that for himself and his little company of friends, poverty was the best condition. In an age which was tremendously intent on money, when even

the Church was more anxious to be rich
than to be holy, there was need of men
who had no interest in wealth. These
men cared nothing for it. They were
glad to be poor. They were happy to be
the brothers of the poor. They went
about begging with the beggars.

One day, in church, Francis heard the
words of Christ to His disciples, telling
them to provide no money for their journey, and to take with them neither shoes,
nor staff, nor wallet, but to go and preach,
saying, "The kingdom of heaven is at
hand." Immediately, he took the words
as meant for him. He cast away his
shoes and his staff; he unloosed the girdle
from which his wallet was suspended, and
finding a rope, tied it about his brown
cloak. Thus the new order was provided
with a uniform. They went with bare
feet, in cloak of brown tied with a rope.
And they began to preach. They jour-
neyed about among the little towns of

Umbria, getting people together in market places, and speaking to them concerning God and their souls.

One of the beautiful stories of the preaching of Francis is about his sermon to the birds. As he was preaching to the people, the birds came and made such a noise chirping to each other in the air that the voice of the speaker could hardly be heard. Then the saint, with his gentle courtesy, turned to the birds. " My sisters," he said, " it is now time that I should speak. Since you have had your say, listen now in your turn to the word of God, and be silent till the sermon is finished." And the legend says that the birds obeyed, and sat still, listening with attention.

Another time, when the number of the disciples of Francis had grown great, and the Little Brothers, as they called themselves, were very many, they held a council at Assisi, in the flowery plain beside

the church of St. Mary of the Angels.
But Francis had made no arrangements
for feeding this multitude of guests. " My
children," he said, "we have promised
great things to God, and greater things
still have we promised to ourselves from
God; let us observe those which we have
promised to Him, and certainly expect
those which are promised to us." And
from all the neighboring towns people
came driving in with food, so that they
had more than enough.

One day Francis said to a young brother
of the company, " Let us go into the town
and preach." So in they went, from St.
Mary's church beside the gate, and
climbed the long Assisi hill, and went
about the streets and markets, and at last
turned their steps towards home having
said never a word. At last the young
man asked, " Father, when do we begin
to preach?" And Francis answered,
" My son, we have been preaching all

the way, for men have seen us as we
went and we have been sermons without
speech. Every man is a sermon every
day."

One dark night Francis and Leo walked
in the cold rain, weary after a long journey, Francis before, Leo behind. And
Francis said, "Brother Leo, if we were
able to give sight to the blind and hearing
to the deaf and recovery to the sick, that
would not be the perfect joy." And
presently Francis said, "Brother Leo, if
we were able to know all knowledge, that
would not be the perfect joy." And, a
while after, Francis said, "Brother Leo,
if we were able to speak with the tongues
of angels, that would not be the perfect
joy." "Well then, Father Francis," said
Leo at last, "what would be the perfect
joy?" And Francis answered, "Here
we come, dripping with rain and shivering with cold, to the monastery of St.
Mary of the Angels, expecting dry clothes,

and warmth and food and sleep. Suppose
the porter does not know us. We knock,
and he says, 'Who is there?' and we answer, 'We are two of thy brethren,' and
he says, 'You are two vagabonds, you are
two tramps,' and out he comes and beats
us, and calls us hard names, and rolls us
in the mud and snow, and goes in, fasten-
ing the door behind him. Then if we get
up and go on in great content, glad to suffer hardships, remembering how our
Master suffered for our sake, that, Brother
Leo, would be the perfect joy."

These stories illustrate the character of
Francis. He was the most gentle, the
most cheerful, the most unselfish of the
saints. In the midst of a time when every
man seemed to be thinking chiefly of his
own advantage, Francis sought no gain
whatever, and desired only to be of service to others. His example revealed the
fact that the world was not so selfish as
it seemed. Not only were there men who

came to live under his rule, but great
numbers of women, beginning with Clara,
a devout young girl of Assisi, who came
from her pleasant home to follow the
brown-gowned brethren, and took up her
residence in that little church of St. Darnian which Francis had rebuilt. And
after her, in the enthusiasm which a holy
life enkindled, came multitudes of men
and women having still their business in the
world, their shops to keep, their children
to bring up, unable to live in the complete
consecration and poverty of Francis and
Clara, and yet most earnestly desiring to
be better. And for them Francis established a third order, giving them simple
rules of devout living which they could
keep in their own homes. Thus the influence of Francis began to touch all the
life about him.

He went to Rome, to ask the blessing
of the pope upon his new society. It is
said that the great Innocent, who had

humbled the king of England, was walking in his garden when Francis appeared, and at first ordered him away, thinking that he was a beggar from the street who had got in by mistake; but it was the pope who was mistaken. Innocent blessed the work of Francis, as he was presently to bless the work of Dominic.

He went even to the remote East, to Egypt and the Holy Land, following the track of the Crusaders, and had an interview with the Sultan. The Sultan was engaged in killing Christians, but Francis was not afraid. In he went and preached his gospel, to which the Sultan listened gravely, and dismissed him in peace.

And year by year, the influence of the self-sacrifice of Francis extended, and the Order grew. One day, the report was brought to him that in a certain city a generous man had given some of his followers a house to live in. He was filled with great grief and alarm. He foresaw that his disciples, devoted to holy poverty and friends of the people because they were poor as the poorest, would by-and-by grow rich like the rest of them, like the men who had followed Benedict, and the men who had followed Bernard. And so indeed it proved. Even in his own lifetime, the beautiful simplicity of the Order began to be changed.

On he went, walking in the steps of Jesus, making his life as near as he could like the perfect life. He went singing, with the love songs of the spirit in place of the love songs of the troubadours. The sun and moon, the hills and lakes, the birds and beasts, he called his brothers and sisters, and made a poem about them, praising God for all the blessings of the world. He was always kind and tender, courteous and gentle; but never sparing himself. Even near the end of his short life, when sickness had begun to overtake him, he would say, " Let us begin over again; up to this moment we have done nothing for God." And it is said that when he died, and they prepared his body to be buried, they found what looked like nail-prints in his hands and feet, and what looked like the mark of a spear in his side, so long and lovingly had he considered the Cross of Christ, and so deeply had he entered into the fellowship of His sufferings.

WYCLIFFE

1320-1384

OLD St. Paul's, in London, was one of the longest of all churches, but it was crowded in all its length and breadth on the day when John Wycliffe was brought there to be tried. Through the narrow lane between the people he made his way from the west door to the chapel behind the altar. Beside him walked the two most powerful men in England, greatest in riches and in influence, and highest in station, Lord Percy and Duke John of Gaunt. Behind him walked the representatives of the four Orders of friars, one for the Order of St. Dominic, one for the Order of St. Francis, two for lesser societies. And behind them came men-at-arms. The archbishop of Canterbury

WYCLIFFE

From a print by G. White, after a picture in the collection
of the Duke of Dorset

was to be the judge; the bishop of London was to be the accuser.

"Sit down, Wycliffe," said Lord Percy, "Since you have much to reply, you will need all the softer seat." "Stand up, Wycliffe," cried the bishop of London. "An accused man may not sit in the presence of the judge." "Nay, but he shall sit," shouted the lord. "Nay, but he shall stand," shouted the bishop. And then the men-at-arms took one side of the dispute, and the townspeople took the other side. And so they fell to fighting. The church was filled with noise and violence. In the midst of the tumult, Wycliffe was carried off in safety.

John Wycliffe was a professor in the University of Oxford. He was the greatest scholar and the greatest preacher of his time. As a scholar he wrote in Latin for the reading of learned men, and proved his points by the complicated logic in which learned men delighted. As a preacher, he spoke in English, plainly, directly, and to the hearts of his hearers. Both in Latin and in English he said things which made all England give attention to him.

Wycliffe attacked the privileges of the Church. He said that the Church was too rich. He found that the temptations of wealth and power, against which Dominic and Francis had done their best, were constantly increasing. Every day the Church was piling up its treasure and extending its land. Even the Dominicans and Franciscans, bound as they were to poverty, were building splendid monasteries and gathering gold as a farmer gathers fruit. It is true that no friar had anything for his own, but the Orders grew rich, and the " little brothers of the poor," as Francis had called them, lived in palaces. The people hated them for their wealth, but still more because, being so rich, they still said that they were poor.

Beside the great houses of the friars, Dominican and Franciscan, were the greater houses of the monks, Benedictine, Cluniac, Cistercian. A third of the land and wealth of England was said to be in the possession of the Church.

Now, at that time, the theory was that the chief business of the Church is to deal on behalf of men with God.

God sat far away upon a vast gold throne, and could be approached only as the king was approached, by His courtiers. Whoever wanted anything of God must get it in this way. They who were engaged in fighting, as most strong men were, could get God on their side, they thought, by keeping the friendship of the Church. So they gave gifts to the clergy; as business men, in places where a city is ruled by a political ring, give gifts to politicians.

The main matter, however, concerning which the Church was believed to have

influence with God was that of punishment for sin. People were continually
taught that they would be punished for
their sins. In almost every church a great
picture of the Last Judgment was painted
on the wall. Michael Angelo's Last Judgment, in the Sistine Chapel, is a familiar
example. The pictures showed the torments of hell. But there was a way of
escape. The Church could save men from
these torments. The process was to confess
one's sins to a priest, to be absolved by
him in the name of God, and to perform
such penance as the priest might direct.
And this help was applied even to those
who had already gone into the world un-
seen. The prayers of the priests were believed to be powerful even for such as
these. They might still be saved from
pain, and helped on into heaven.

Thus men and women employed the
services of the Church both for themselves
and for their friends. They gave lands,

built churches, and paid money according to their means, in order to save themselves and those whom they loved from the distress of punishment for sin in the world to come. The value of the Church was thought to consist, not in its relation to this present life, helping people to be better, but in its relation to the future life. The theory that sin could be committed without fear of punishment by paying the Church to save the sinner from the pain which he deserved, encouraged men in sin. The principal business of a man of religion,—a priest, a monk, or a friar,— was to say prayers. The purpose of the Church was not so much to change the will of men, making them better, as to change the will of God, making Him more kind to sinners. And the great wealth which the Church got in payment for these services was spent upon the Church. The people got nothing back but prayers.

It was for speaking against all this that Wycliffe had been brought to trial. The one thing plain at that moment to his mind was that the Church was injured by its wealth. He felt, like Dominic and Francis, that poverty was essential to religion. What they meant was that a self-seeking Church, getting everything and giving nothing, was in no position to do its true work in the world. Wycliffe proposed that the property of the Church be taken away. That was the best solution he could think of. And Lord Percy and Duke John of Gaunt agreed with him most heartily; for when the property of the Church was taken away they hoped to get a large share of it for themselves.

All this social preaching of Wycliffe, wise or unwise, was suddenly stopped by the Peasants' Revolt. All over England, the poor arose against the rich. The times were hard and people were hungry. The situation was embittered by a long and unsuccessful war with France, for whose heavy and foolish expenses the land was taxed. Then came John Ball and Wat Tyler and other leaders, and burned castles, and invaded London. And their attack was directed, not only against the rich towns, but against the rich monasteries. The archbishop of Canterbury, who was to have judged Wycliffe in St. Paul's, they killed, and they would have killed John of Gaunt also if they could have caught him. It was made plain that all wealth, whether held by laymen or by churchmen, was in peril. Any attack upon it, even with the best of motives, was likely to be like a lighted match beside a magazine of powder. The Peasants' Revolt stopped the assault of Wycliffe upon the bad wealth of the Church.

He turned his attention to bad doctrine.

It became plain to Wycliffe that the power and the wealth which were destroying the spiritual life of the Church were due to the evil influences of a mistaken doctrine of the Lord's Supper. According to this doctrine, the pronouncing of certain words by a priest in the service had the effect of bringing Christ to the altar at which he ministered. The bread of the Supper was changed by the priest's words into the body of Christ, and the wine into the blood of Christ. Thus the priest brought God down out of heaven. The miracle proved the priest's power with God. This power he could turn for or against men as he chose. He could save men from the punishment of their sins, or he could condemn them to everlasting torment. His blessing was the blessing of heaven; his curse was the curse of hell.

This doctrine Wycliffe denied. In his lecture room at Oxford he showed his pupils that it had no foundation in Scripture or in reason. The bread of the sacrament was bread still, the wine was wine still. The presence of Christ was a spiritual presence. As for the excommunications of the Church, they are of effect, he said, only when they are deserved. The way to be saved is not by sacraments but by godly living. Every man may come straight to God without the aid of any priest.

The new teaching startled the country. John of Gaunt hurried down to Oxford to tell Wycliffe that he could expect no protection from the court for such ideas as these. The pope sent word from Rome to have the preacher silenced. But Wycliffe replied to John of Gaunt that he proposed to follow truth wherever it might lead him. As for the pope, he said that the Greek Church got on very well without any pope, and he thought the Latin Church might do the same.

They held a council against him in London and condemned his teachings. But in the afternoon, while the churchmen were busy pointing out his errors, there came a tremendous earthquake. The whole house in which they sat was shaken, church steeples fell, and towers of castles were destroyed. The effect of this singular coincidence was to strengthen the influence of Wycliffe. He was, indeed, dismissed from his professorship at Oxford; but he retired to his parish at Lutterworth, and there continued both to write and to preach.

The little parish became the center of the new movement. Wycliffe took up the work of Dominic and Francis. Dominic had tried to save the Church by the preaching of the truth; the Dominicans were to reason with heretics. But the plan had failed, and instead of convincing men by reason the endeavor was made to compel them by torture. Francis had tried to

save the Church by living a life of love.
But his example was followed only for
a little while. The time came when the
Franciscans who desired to live like
Francis were persecuted by the Franciscans who desired to live more comfortably.
Wycliffe sent out men from Lutterworth
to save the Church by attacking the posi-
tions which made the Church strong as
an institution but weak as an influence
for good. These men, clad in long
russet gowns, and called Lollards, carried in their hands pages of the English
Bible.

Wycliffe, in his quiet rectory of Lutterworth, had translated the Bible. He had
taken it over from the Latin of Jerome,
and had made it speak the common speech
of the people. That speech would sound
strange in our ears. The English language
had not yet come into the form which we
have it now. Chaucer, about the same
time, was writing the Canterbury Tales.

A glance at Chaucer's pages shows how like his English was to ours, and yet how very different. But that was how men spoke. And when the Bible was read to them in those words, they understood it. That was what Wycliffe wanted. He believed that what was needed to save the Church was an understanding of the Bible, and a return to the spirit of the Bible. " Here," cried the Lollards in the market-places, " here is God's truth in God's book. Where are the priests, where are the penances, where the images of the saints, where are the prayers for the dead, where is the ritual of the sacrament of the altar, where is the pope, in God's book? "

Wycliffe died in peace, being taken with his last illness in the midst of a service in his church. Half a century later, his enemies dug up his body and burned it, and cast the ashes upon the surface of the little river Swift. And the

Swift, as his friends said, bore them to the Severn, and the Severn to the sea. It was a symbol of the spread of Wycliffe's influence. For Wycliffe was the beginner of the English Reformation.

HUS

1373-1415

THE splendid hope of Hildebrand and
Innocent that the bishop of Rome would
make the bad world good, had come to
naught. They had dreamed of a great
pope ministering to the nations as a pastor
ministers to his people, correcting the
wrong and commending the right, having
moral authority over kings, and making
peace in the place of war. They felt that
what Europe needed was the control of a
strong, wise, and good man.

Unhappily, for three hundred years,
from the beginning of the thirteenth century to the beginning of the sixteenth,
hardly a pope was either strong, or wise,
or good. Some were politicians, who
made bargains for money and power with
kings. Some were well-meaning but weak

JOHN HUS
From the Herrenhut Archives

men. Some were persons whose wicked lives were a scandal to religion; thieves, adulterers, and murderers.

At the beginning of the fourteenth century, the pope moved from Italy to France, from Rome to Avignon. There he lived under the control of the French king. At the end of that century, on the occasion of a papal election, the cardinals chose an Italian, who took up his residence in Rome. He proved, however, to be so bad a pope that they immediately chose another, who took up his residence in Avignon. So there were two popes. A part of the Church held with the one, another part with the other. The two fought with curses, exchanging excommunications. Wycliffe compared them to two dogs snarling and growling over a bone. This state of things continued for nearly forty years.

At last a council was held which declared that a general conference of Christian men representing the Church is superior to all popes. An attempt was made to get both popes to resign for the good of the Church. When they refused, the council put them both out, and chose another, Alexander V. He died after a short time, and John XXIII., who is thought to have poisoned him, became pope in his place. Thus, although two scandals were amended,—the scandal of the papal court at Avignon, and the scandal of the papal schism,—the worst of the scandals remained: the pope was still a man of wicked life.

John XXIII. is said to have begun his career as a pirate. The record of his misdeeds was such that before it was read to the Council which finally deposed him, all outsiders were put out and the doors were locked. It was John who began that public and shameless sale of indulgences which hastened the Reformation. He conceived the ingenious idea of making

money by sending agents all over Europe
who promised to release sinners from the
punishment due to their sins on the payment of certain specified prices. Of
course, there were still good Christians.
There were faithful ministers who lived
devout lives, and tried to help their people
to do right. But the great Church, as
represented by the pope at the head, and
by the bishops, the monks, and the friars,
was teaching men, by constant example,
to break the Ten Commandments.

It was against this dreadful situation
that Wycliffe had protested, but the
remedies which he had proposed seemed
as bad as the disease. When he said that
the trouble with the Church was wealth
and power, many agreed; but when he
proposed to take away the wealth by
giving up the property of the Church, and
to take away the power by giving up the
doctrine of the miracle of the Body and
Blood, they would not follow him.

Neither would they follow Hus.

John Hus was a professor in the University of Prague, and the greatest preacher in that part of the country. Born on a farm, and getting his education in spite of such poverty that he begged in the street, Hus had made himself a scholar and a leader. He was a man of simple mind, and righteous life and plain speech. He saw the evils in the Church about him, and made it the business of his life to put an end to them. The books of Wycliffe came to his knowledge and he liked them greatly.

Now, there are two ways in which to deal with evil. One way is to attack in general, without making mention of any names. The other way is to attack it in particular, singling out certain offenders and denouncing them. The first way is easy and safe; the second is full of danger. Hus took the second way.

For example, at the town of Wilsnack,

the priests of one of the churches had announced a miracle. They said that it was now proved that the bread in the Lord's Supper is indeed the Body of Christ because pieces of it on their altar had shed blood. And the Holy Blood of Wilsnack began to work miracles. Pilgrims came from all directions, bringing their sick, to the great advantage of the Wilsnack church. Hus was sent to look into the matter, and he found that it was all a fraud. The result was that the pilgrimages to Wilsnack stopped. But the Wilsnack clergy hated Hus.

And other clergy, for like reasons, hated him. The man was absolutely outspoken. He had no " tact," as we say. He never considered whether his words would have a pleasant sound or not. He paid no heed to his own interest. Every day, he made enemies. At that time the most unpopular name in Europe was that of Wycliffe. He was much more disliked by many people than the scandalous popes who were busy breaking the commandments. Hus approved of him. He did not go with all the attacks which Wycliffe made on church doctrine, but he liked every word which Wycliffe said about the wicked lives of churchmen. And he said so openly. At a time when bishops were burning Wycliffe's books, Hus was reading them and praising them. He was saying in Prague what Wycliffe had said at Oxford.

Hus was therefore summoned by his enemies to defend himself before the council which was called to meet at Constance. Over this council the Emperor Sigismund was to preside. Hus in his simplicity and innocence, knowing himself to be opposed to nothing in the Church except its sins, agreed to appear before the council, and the emperor gave him a safe-conduct. This was a paper signed by the emperor himself promising that Hus should be safe from violence and should be brought back from the council to his home by the emperor's own guard, if necessary. Thus he went.

The council immediately arrested Hus, and put him in prison. They paid no heed to the safe-conduct of the emperor, and the emperor, on his side, made no serious protest. The theory was that any man accused of heresy was to be accounted a heretic until he had proved himself innocent, and that no faith was to be kept with heretics. No matter what promises had been made, what safe-conducts given, what oaths solemnly sworn, all went for nothing in the case of a heretic.

So Hus was put in prison before his trial had begun, and then was moved to another prison where he was chained by the arms in the daytime and by the arms and legs at night. These were some of the more gentle measures of the Inquisition.

When he was brought at last before the council, he was hooted down whenever

he began to speak. Charges were read
against him; passages were taken from his
books and from the books of Wycliffe,
which were held to be against the faith
and order of the Church. Some of these
he denied as not expressing his beliefs;
some he said he would gladly change if
anybody could show him that they were
not true. He refused to change any
opinion by reason of compulsion. He
declared the independence of man's conscience, and held that belief is a matter
of persuasion and conviction, not of
authority.

This was his chief fault. He had won
the hatred of the Church by his free
speech concerning the sins of churchmen;
he was condemned and sentenced because
he maintained the right of a man who is
in error to be shown his error. His only
error was that of insisting that a Christian
minister, even a pope, ought to be a good
man. That that was an error, nobody

could convince him. As for heresy, he had none of it.

Nevertheless, they condemned him to be burned. That was the answer of the council to the man who tried to bring back into the Church the plain righteousness of true religion. They agreed that the Church needed to be reformed, and had assembled for the purpose of reforming it. But they did not like John Hus's way.

They degraded him from the ministry, dressing him in the garments of a priest, and putting a chalice and paten in his hand, and then taking them away with curses. "We commit thy soul," they said, " to the devil." "And I commit it," he answered, " to the most sacred Lord Jesus Christ."

Then they put a paper cap upon his head, with a writing on it saying that he died for heresy. He was taken out and tied to a stake, with a chain about his neck. Fagots were heaped about him, and he was burned to death.

SAVONAROLA

1452-1498

THE monastery of San Marco in Florence faces a quiet square, and is adorned with the paintings of Fra Angelico. There is the picture of the two disciples who invite the Lord to come and be their guest, and the picture of the brother with his finger on his lips in symbol of silence. In every cell is painted a Madonna, or a crucifix, or the figure of an angel, to help the prayers of the friars of St. Dominic. In one cell, somewhat apart from the others, meant for the prior, are treasured a desk at which Savonarola wrote and a chair in which he sat, and a portrait of him hangs upon the wall.

Savonarola had intended to be a doctor, like his grandfather; though even as a lad he was interested in theology, and looked

HIERONYMI·FERRARIENSIS·A·DEO·
✕·MISSI·PROPHETÆ·EFFIGIES✕

SAVONAROLA

From the picture by Fra Bartolommeo, San Marco, Florence

out upon the world with serious eyes. At the age of nineteen, he was deeply in love with a girl whose parents would not allow her to marry him. His family, they said, was not so good as hers. This made him more serious still. He had never cared for the pleasures of society; now he hated them. He wrote an essay about this time, entitled, " Contempt of the World."

It was a bad world; that was plain even to a young man of nineteen. What Hus saw in the streets of Prague, Savonarola saw in the streets of Ferrara. There were pride and oppression, vice and drunkenness, men fighting with sharp swords and women looking on applauding, and no peace or order. Savonarola separated himself from it. He entered a monastery and became a Dominican. Presently he was sent to live in Florence with the brothers of San Marco.

The ruler of Florence was Lorenzo, called " the Magnificent." Under his government all bad things were growing in the city like weeds on a neglected farm. Lorenzo was intent on power and money, and cared little how he got them. With all his splendid titles, his robes of state and his palace, he was like the political bosses, who to-day get control of cities, throw open all the doors of wickedness, and tax honest citizens for their own advantage.

It was found that the new brother at San Marco could preach. Not very well, it seemed at first, when he took commonplace texts and treated them in commonplace ways. But one day, as he spoke in the pulpit concerning the Day of Judgment, a sudden inspiration came upon him. He denounced the sins of men in the light of the flames of that awful day of punishment, till his hearers wept and trembled. Afterwards they said that they saw a halo gleaming round his head.

And then, as he preached again, he had

a vision of a flaming sword, and heard
voices promising the mercy of God to the
faithful and the wrath of God to the un-
faithful, and, as he looked, the sword was
lifted against the earth amidst the flash
of lightnings and the crash of thunders.

With this new eloquence, in the spirit
of the Day of Judgment, Savonarola attacked the city government of Florence.
He took his texts out of the Bible, and
mainly from the prophets of the Old
Testament, but in every text he succeeded
in finding something against Lorenzo the
Magnificent

He was made prior of the monastery.
It was a bold election, not only because
some of the chief citizens had protested
against his sermons, but because Lorenzo
was the great patron of San Marco. The
monastery had been rebuilt by his father,
and he himself had enriched and adorned
it. Suppose, now, that the richest, most
generous, and most influential person in

the parish is at the same time an unscrupulous political boss and a man of evil life; what shall the parson do? That was the question which confronted the new prior, and he answered by continuing his sermons against Lorenzo.

When Lorenzo lay upon his deathbed, he sent for Savonarola. He knew that there was one fearless and honest minister in Florence, and he wished his counsel in the preparation of his soul. Savonarola said, "You must repent, and trust in the mercy of God." To this Lorenzo assented. "You must give up the wealth which you have taken by dishonest means." To this also, after some hesitation, he assented. "You must restore the liberties of Florence." Then Lorenzo turned his face to the wall, and made no answer, and the prior in silence came away.

The liberties of Florence were restored by Savonarola. In the confusion which followed the death of Lorenzo, the prior was chosen as the natural leader of the decent citizens. The king of France was fighting the king of Naples. Down he came with his army, and entered Florence; and out he went again, by reason of the moral strength of Savonarola. When the king threatened the city, saying, " I will sound my trumpets," it was in the spirit of Savonarola that Capponi answered, "Then we will ring our bells."

Thus Savonarola prevailed in Florence. He drew up a new plan of government by which the magistrates were bound to the fear of God and the purification of manners, and to promote the public welfare in preference to private interests. Jesus Christ was solemnly proclaimed the king of Florence. People put off their gay clothes, and dressed soberly. Hymns took the place of the popular songs. One day, men and women brought their " vanities," their fine apparel, their adornments, and burned them in a great bonfire, while the

Dominicans of San Marco, hand in hand, danced about the flames, to the glory of God.

But there were enemies. There were many people whose hearts were not touched by the preaching of Savonarola, and who disliked all this new plainness and simplicity. They honestly hated hymns, and desired the open doors of Lorenzo's time. There were also the Franciscans, who were jealous of the popularity of the Dominicans. And there was the pope.

The very name of the family to which the pope of that day belonged, is a synonym of shameless evil. He was a Borgia. He had abandoned all righteousness, and was suspected of having abandoned all Christian faith as well. He was a criminal and a heretic, and yet the pope. Savonarola denounced him, as he had denounced Lorenzo.

But the pope was possessed of all the power of great wealth and great position.

He could bribe with one hand, and curse
with the other. Powerful as he was, he
yet saw that it was not safe to let himself be publicly abused by popular preachers. There were too many people who
would listen to such preaching eagerly.
The Middle Ages were drawing to a
close. Already new ideas were beginning
to stir the minds of men. The fall of
Constantinople at the hands of the Turks,
in 1453, had sent fugitive Greek scholars
into Europe, and men were beginning to
read the Greek Testament, with new
understanding. The discovery of America,
in 1492, was disclosing the greatness
of the world; the invention of printing was making it possible for plain
men to read books for themselves,
and make up their own minds. The
invention of powder was putting a
new strength into the arms of peasants.
The protests of the Albigenses, of the Lollards, of the Hussites, were revealing an

increasing unrest in the face of the sins
of churchmen. Reforming councils were
deposing even popes. Alexander Borgia
was afraid to allow Savonarola to preach
his fierce sermons. People were so interested in them that they crowded the
cathedral before the sun was up, on
preaching days, each with his lighted
candle.

Then all the enemies fell upon the
prior. The pope excommunicated him.
The Franciscans proposed a trial by fire,
according to an ancient custom: a Franciscan on one side, and a Dominican on the
other, were to walk across the wide square
between rows of blazing fagots, and the
one who got through safely would be
proved to be in the right. The rows
of fagots were built, and all Florence was
there to see. But the Franciscans, though
it was their champion who would not
venture, contrived to put the blame on
the Dominicans. Savonarola and his friars,

as they marched back to San Marco, were hooted and stoned. It was evident that his righteous power was broken.

The monastery was stormed by a mob. The doors were broken down; citizens and friars fought together. Fra Domenico, Savonarola's faithful friend, defended the prior with a huge candlestick, which he wielded like a club. But Savonarola was arrested, and Domenico with him, and another also, named Silvestro. They were tried, as the manner was, by torture, and condemned. "I separate thee," said the bishop, "from the Church militant and from the Church triumphant." "Not from the Church triumphant," said the martyr: "That is beyond thy power."

A bronze tablet in the pavement of the great square of Florence shows where Savonarola and his friends were first hanged and then burned for their attack upon the wickedness of the world and of the Church.

Thus passes the procession of our twenty saints and heroes. The list ends with a martyr, as it began. And every man came into acquaintance with difficulty and danger. They might have lived in peace and comfort like their neighbors, but they had a strong longing to do good. They entered with great joy into the old war between wrong and right. That war is as new as it is old: it is going on in our neighborhood to-day. Indeed, we are all enlisted in it, on one side or the other.

THE END